CHAMBERS

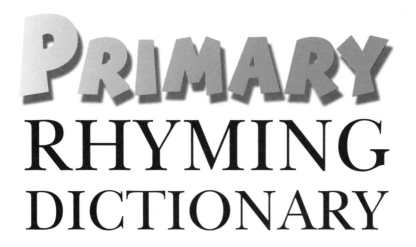

RHYMING
DICTIONARY

CHAMBERS

CHAMBERS
An imprint of Chambers Harrap Publishers Ltd
7 Hopetoun Crescent
Edinburgh, EH7 4AY

First published by Chambers Harrap Publishers Ltd 2004

A CIP catalogue record for this book is available from the British Library.

ISBN 0550 10089 X

Designed and typeset by Chambers Harrap Publishers Ltd, Edinburgh
Printed and bound in France by Partenaires

Contents

Contributors

Project Editor
Mary O'Neill

Compiler
Alice Grandison

Poems
Benjamin Zephaniah

Illustrations
John-Paul Early

Editorial Assistance
Helen Bleck

Publishing Manager
Patrick White

Prepress
Vienna Leigh
Sharon McTeir

The editors would like to acknowledge with thanks the assistance and advice of the following:

Bruntsfield Primary School, Edinburgh

Cloudside Junior School, Sandiacre, Derbyshire

Higher Bebington Junior School, Bebington, Wirral

Holden Lane Primary School, Stoke-on-Trent, Staffordshire

Maltman's Green School, Gerrards Cross, Buckinghamshire

New Cangle CP School, Haverhill, Suffolk

Whitehills Lower School, Kingsthorpe, Northampton

Preface

Chambers Primary Rhyming Dictionary has been specially compiled for use by primary school pupils aged 7-11, at Key Stage 2 of the English and Welsh National Curriculum and levels C and D of Curriculum and Assessment in Scotland.

The aim of the dictionary is to provide pupils at this level with all the words they need to express themselves with creative rhymes. Over 400 groups of rhymes give over 8000 potential rhyming words for children to use, from simple terms to more challenging words for older or more able primary pupils, and all in a colourful and easy-to-use format. Within these larger groups, words are organized into smaller sections according to the spelling of the rhyming sound. This way, rhyming can help increase phonic awareness by encouraging recognition of the relationships between sound and spelling.

The words in 60 of the sections are brought to vibrant life with verses by the poet Benjamin Zephaniah, all featured in eye-catching boxes. Ranging in structure from couplets to limericks, and in tone from reflective through lighthearted to the comically absurd, his poems are sure to appeal to children and demonstrate to them the fun they can have with rhyming words.

In addition, 30 of the poems are accompanied by dynamic and often humorous illustrations which bring another dimension to the poems and further enliven the book.

We hope that *Chambers Primary Rhyming Dictionary* will prove an invaluable resource for primary school pupils being introduced to the joys of poetry and rhyme.

www

To help make best use of Chambers Primary titles, teachers can download photocopiable games and exercises from our website at
www.chambers.co.uk

All about rhyme

What is rhyme?

Rhyme is when two words end in a similar sound.

Rhyme is used everywhere. You hear it in songs, in slogans and jingles in advertisements, in popular sayings and proverbs, and of course in poems.

A poem does not have to rhyme, but sometimes rhyme makes people take notice of it, and helps them to remember it.

Types of rhyme

True rhyme is where a word ends in exactly the same sound as another, for example:

> He could twist through the **air**
> And land straight on a ch**air**

However, you can make rhymes with words where the vowels are the same, but the consonants are slightly different. This is called half-rhyme.

This means that you can pick words from other groups in this book for your rhyme if the sound is quite similar. An example of a half-rhyme is:

> When the sun c**ame** they danced ag**ain**

This example also shows you that a line of poetry can have a rhyme within it. This is called internal rhyme. Here is another example:

> Normally I get my k**icks** writing silly limer**icks**

In a perfect rhyme the words have a different consonant before the final, rhyming sound.

> He played and made an awful **drone**
> And now poor Frederick lives a**lone**.

In an imperfect rhyme the words have the same consonant before the rhyming sound, for example:

> When folk get old I do ob**serve**
> They get the face that they de**serve**.

Types of poem using rhyme

There are many types of poem where rhyme is used. You might like to try writing some of your own.

Many of you will have heard funny poems called limericks. A limerick always has five lines. The first two lines rhyme with each other, then the next two lines rhyme with each other, and the final line rhymes with the first one:

> A schoolteacher made out of plastic
> Was quite flexible and gymnastic,
> He could twist through the air
> And land straight on a chair,
> All the kids thought his feet were fantastic.

Another type of verse is called a rhyming couplet. A rhyming couplet is two lines that rhyme beside each other, without any lines in between, for example:

> They say to play in pantomime
> It helps if you turn up on time.

How do I use my Rhyming Dictionary?

Imagine you are writing a poem about a bear, and want to find a word that rhymes with bear. There are two ways you can do this.

1. Look up the word in the index

The first way is go to the index at the back of the book. The index is a list of all the rhyming words in this book, in alphabetical order.

Look up the word bear in the index.

This tells you where you will find the word bear – the section that has the big heading -are as the rhyming sound.

Go to the rhyming sound section in the book with -are at the top. All the rhyming sounds are in alphabetical order so you can easily find them.

Here you will find words that rhyme with bear.

2. Look up the rhyming sound in the book

The second way to find rhyming words is to go straight to the pages of the book to look up the part of your word that is the rhyming sound. This part always begins with a vowel - a, e, i, o or u – or with y.

First of all, you have to decide which part of the word is the rhyming sound. You do this by listening for the part you stress the most when you are speaking, because this is where the rhyme is. This means that in the word clever the rhyming sound is not -er, because this part does not have any stress. The rhyming sound is -ever.

It is much easier to work out the rhyming part in a short word such as bear – the rhyming sound is -ear.

All the rhyming sounds are in alphabetical order, so you can look this part up quite easily.

Sometimes the words you are looking for will be in the first place you look. However, sometimes the words will be elsewhere. For example, at -ear you will see this:

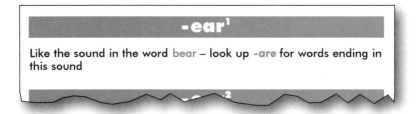

-ear[1]

Like the sound in the word bear – look up -are for words ending in this sound

This tells you to go to the section of rhyming sounds headed -are to find the rhyming words you want.

If the rhyming words you want are not in the first place you looked, and there is no note telling you where they are instead, then use the index at the back of the book to find them.

Different rhyming sounds with the same spelling

Sometimes a spelling can have more than one sound. -ear, for instance, can be pronounced like the sound in the word bear, or like the sound in the word ear.

This is why you might see a section with the same heading as the following one. These headings have numbers alongside them to show you they have different rhyming sounds.

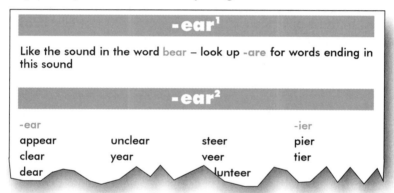

-ear[1]

Like the sound in the word bear – look up -are for words ending in this sound

-ear[2]

-ear			-ier
appear	unclear	steer	pier
clear	year	veer	tier
dear		...lunteer	

Different spellings with the same rhyming sound

You will see that the rhyming words for each sound are sometimes divided into groups. The rhyming sound is spelled a different way in each group of words. The red heading above each smaller group shows you the way the sound is spelled in each one.

-ur

-ur	-er	-ir	-irr
blur	deter	fir	whirr
fur	her	sir	
occur	prefer	stir	-urr
slur	refer		purr
spur	transfer	-ere	
		were	-yrrh
			myrrh

You can use any word you like as a rhyme, because even if it is spelled differently, it sounds the same.

Because people from different parts of the country pronounce words in different ways, there may be some words in the rhyming groups that you do not think rhyme with each other. There may be other rhymes you would use instead.

It is all right to use the words you think rhyme with each other, even if they are not in the same section in the book! Benjamin Zephaniah himself encourages would-be poets to break the rules. He said, 'there are no boundaries to the things that you can do in poetry'.

Words with no rhyme

If you think of a word in English, you will usually be able to think of other words that rhyme with it. However, there are some words that do not have rhymes. The most famous one is orange.

Here are some others. Can you think of any more?

angel
burger
circle
friendly
good-natured
pint
temple

-ab

-ab

blab	kebab	scab	stab
cab	lab	slab	tab
crab	minicab		
dab			
drab			
fab			
grab			
jab			

Here you'll find rhymes that are *fab*
Rhymes that are up for the *grab*,
So relax as you sit at your table
And rhyme like mad as you are now able.

-abby

-abby

		-abbie	-abbey
crabby	flabby	Abbie	abbey
fabby	tabby	cabbie	

-able

-able

			-abel
able	enable	timetable	label
cable	fable	unable	Mabel
coffee table	gable	unstable	
dinner table	stable		
disable	table		

-ace

-ace

ace
at a snail's pace
brace
disgrace
face
face-to-face
Grace
grace
in-your-face
lace
make a face
marketplace
misplace

not a hair out of place
pace
place
pull a face
race
replace
slap in the face
space
trace
unlace
waste of space

-ase

base
briefcase
case
chase
database
pillowcase
suitcase
wild-goose chase

-aice

plaice (= a fish)

-ass

bass (= a low sound)

-aced

-aced

baby-faced
disgraced
faced
laced
misplaced
paced
placed

raced
red-faced
replaced
straitlaced
traced
unlaced

-aste

cut-and-paste
haste
paste
taste
toothpaste
waste

-ased

based
chased

-aist

waist

-acing

-acing

bracing
facing
gracing
lacing

misplacing
pacing
placing
racing

replacing
spacing
tracing

-asing

chasing

-ack

-ack		-ak	-ac
attack		anorak	almanac
back	quack	yak (= a type	Tic-tac®
backpack	rack	of ox with	zodiac
black	sack	long hair)	
crack	shack		
get your own	slack		
back	smack		
hardback	snack		
Jack	stack		
knack	tack		
lack	track		
laid-back	unpack		
pack	whack		
paperback	yack (= to		
piggyback	talk)		
pitch-black			

-acked

Look up -act for words ending in this sound

-acks

-acks		-ax	-aks
attacks	shacks	climax	anoraks
backpacks	slacks	fax	yaks
backs	smacks	Halifax	
cracks	snacks	relax	-acs
hardbacks	stacks	wax	Tic-tacs®
packs	tacks		
paperbacks	tracks		-axe
racks	unpacks		axe
sacks	whacks		

3

-act

-act		-acked	
abstract	extract	attacked	tracked
act	fact	backed	unpacked
attract	impact	cracked	whacked
caught in the act	intact	jam-packed	yacked
compact	matter of fact	lacked	
contact	overreact	packed	
contract	pact	quacked	
distract	react	sacked	
exact	subtract	smacked	
	tact	stacked	

-action

-action

action	distraction	reaction	transaction
attraction	extraction	satisfaction	
contraction	fraction	subtraction	

-actor

-actor

actor	factor	tractor
contractor	protractor	

-ad

-ad			-add
ad	fad	like mad	add
bad	glad	mad	
Baghdad	grandad	pad	
barking mad	had	sad	
Brad	hopping mad		
dad	lad		

-ade

-ade

arcade
blade
brigade
degrade
fade
fire brigade
grade
grenade
handmade
home-made
invade
Jade
lampshade
lemonade
made
man-made
marmalade
parade
persuade
razor blade
rollerblade
serenade
shade
spade

sunshade
tailor-made
trade
wade
well-made

-aid

afraid
aid
barmaid
braid
bridesmaid
chambermaid
first aid
laid
maid

mislaid
paid
raid
unpaid
well-paid

-ayed

betrayed
decayed
delayed
displayed
played
portrayed
prayed
sprayed
stayed

swayed

-eyed

conveyed
disobeyed
obeyed

-eighed

neighed
weighed

-ede

suede

-ey'd

they'd

> I kissed my sweetheart Julie
> As we sat in the **shade**,
> The sun was so hot so we
> Drank ice-cool **lemonade**.

-aded

-aded

degraded
faded
invaded
jaded

persuaded
shaded
traded
waded

-aided

aided
braided
raided
unaided

-ading

-ading

		-aiding
degrading	rollerblading	aiding
fading	serenading	braiding
grading	shading	raiding
invading	trading	
persuading	wading	

-aft

-aft		-aughed	-aught
aircraft	handicraft	laughed	draught
art and craft	hovercraft		
craft	needlecraft		
daft	raft		
graft	shaft		

-ag

-ag

bag	gasbag	nag	stag
brag	hag	rag	tag
drag	handbag	saddlebag	wag
fag	jag	sag	
flag	lose your rag	scallywag	
gag	mag	snag	

-age

-age

age	offstage	rattle	upstage
backstage	on-stage	someone's cage	wage
cage	over-age	stage	
engage	page	under-age	**-auge**
enrage	rage		gauge

-aging

-aging

caging	raging	upstaging	-ageing
paging	staging		ageing

-aid

Look up -ade for words ending in this sound

-ail

-ail		-ale	
ail	ponytail	ale	sale
bail	quail	exhale	scale
blackmail	rail	fairytale	stale
fail	sail	female	tale
fight tooth and	snail	full-scale	whale
nail	tail	gale	
fingernail	toenail	inhale	-eil
frail	trail	large-scale	unveil
Gail	wail	male	veil
hail	without fail	nightingale	
jail		pale	-aille
mail			Braille
nail			
pail	*Will I go to jail*		-ey'll
pigtail	*If I fight tooth and nail?*		they'll

-ailer

-ailer	-aler	-ailor
blackmailer	inhaler	sailor
jailer	paler	tailor
trailer	whaler	
wailer		

-ailing

-ailing
ailing
blackmailing
failing
mailing
plain sailing

railing
sailing
trailing
unfailing
wailing

-aling
exhaling
inhaling
scaling
whaling

-eiling
unveiling

-ain

-ain
abstain
birdbrain
brain
chain
complain
contain
detain
disdain
down the drain
drain
entertain
explain
gain
grain
lain
main
maintain
obtain
pain
plain
rain
remain
restrain
retain

right as rain
scatterbrain
Spain
sprain
stain
strain
train
vain

-ane
aeroplane
cane
Cellophane®
crane
Dane
humane
hurricane
insane
Jane
lane
mane
pane
plane
sane

Shane
vane
wane
windowpane

-ein
rein
vein

-agne
champagne

-aign
campaign

-aine
Lorraine

-ayne
Wayne

-eign
reign

-ained

-ained

			-aigned
abstained	house-trained	retained	campaigned
chained	maintained	sprained	
complained	obtained	stained	-eigned
contained	pained	strained	reigned
detained	potty-trained	toilet-trained	
entertained	rained	trained	
explained	remained	unexplained	
gained	restrained	untrained	

-ainer

-ainer

		-aigner	-aner
complainer	strainer	campaigner	saner
container	trainer		
entertainer	vainer		
plainer			

-aining

-aining

abstaining	entertaining	obtaining	restraining
complaining	explaining	potty-training	retaining
containing	gaining	raining	straining
detaining	maintaining	remaining	toilet-training
			training

*The school needs **maintaining**
And so I'm **campaigning**
Troublemaking and faking I ain't,
It leaks when it's **raining**
The pigeons need **training**
And the walls need a large drop of paint.*

-aigning
campaigning

-eigning
reigning

9

-aint

-aint

complaint
faint
paint

quaint
repaint
saint

spray-paint
taint

-ain't

ain't

-air

Look up -are for words ending in this sound

-airy

Look up -ary for words ending in this sound

-ake

-ake

awake
bake
brake
cake
cheesecake
drake
fake
flake
for goodness'
 sake
give-and-take
handbrake
lake
make
mistake
namesake

overtake
pancake
quake
rake
rattlesnake
remake
retake
sake
shake
snake
stake
take
undertake
wake

-ache

ache
backache
headache
heartache
stomachache
tummyache

-eak

break
heartbreak
steak

-aken

-aken
awaken
mistaken
overtaken
reawaken
shaken
taken
waken

-acon
bacon
streaky bacon

-aican
Jamaican

> They danced to reggae in the rain
> The earth and sky were **shaken**,
> When the sun came they danced again
> Of course they were **Jamaican**.

-aker

-aker
baker
caretaker
dressmaker
holidaymaker
lawmaker
maker
matchmaker

pacemaker
Quaker
shoemaker
taker
troublemaker
undertaker

-eaker
breaker
heartbreaker
housebreaker

-acre
acre

-aica
Jamaica

-aking

-aking
awaking
baking
braking
breathtaking
decision-
  making
dressmaking
faking
flaking
in the making

making
mistaking
moneymaking
overtaking
painstaking
profit-
  making
quaking
raking
remaking

retaking
shaking
taking
troublemaking
waking

-eaking
backbreaking
breaking
ground-
  breaking
heartbreaking
housebreaking
recordbreaking

-aching
aching

-ale

Look up -ail for words ending in this sound

-ality

-ality

brutality	personality
formality	practicality
hospitality	punctuality
immortality	reality
informality	speciality
legality	technicality
locality	vitality
morality	
nationality	
normality	
originality	

> The truth is, in *reality*
> The bully spreads *brutality*.

-alk

-alk	-ork	-awk
catwalk	cork	hawk
chalk	New York	squawk
stalk	pork	tomahawk
talk	stork	
walk	York	

-alker

-alker		-orca
hillwalker	talker	Majorca
sleepwalker	walker	Minorca

-alking

-alking

hillwalking   smooth-talking   talking   walking

-all

-all		-awl	-aul
all	mall	bawl	haul
ball	overall	brawl	Paul
basketball	rainfall	crawl	
call	recall	drawl	-al
cannonball	small	scrawl	appal
fall	stall	shawl	
football	tall	sprawl	
free-for-all	volleyball	trawl	
hall	wall		
handball	waterfall		
install			

-alling

-alling	-awling	-auling
appalling	bawling	hauling
calling	brawling	
enthralling	crawling	
falling	drawling	
galling	scrawling	
installing	sprawling	
name-calling	trawling	
recalling		
stalling		

My brother Paul was playing football
But his playing was really **appalling**,
He tried to stand tall but he felt very small
When the crowd started all their **name-calling**.

-ally

-ally	-alley	-ali
dally	alley	Ali
rally	galley	
Sally	valley	

-alm

Like the sound in the word calm – look up -arm[1] for words ending in this sound

-alter

-alter	-alta	-altar
alter	Malta	altar
falter		
halter		

-am

-am			-amme
am	ham	ram	centigramme
Amsterdam	jam	Sam	gramme
anagram	hologram	scram	kilogramme
centigram	kilogram	slam	milligramme
clam	milligram	swam	programme
cram	pram		
dam	program (=		-amb
diagram	computer		lamb
exam	program)		
gram	RAM		

-ame

-ame			-aim
became	lame	tame	aim
blame	much the	what's-her-	claim
came	same	name	exclaim
dame	name	what's-his-	maim
fame	overcame	name	proclaim
flame	put to shame	what's-its-	
frame	same	name	
game	shame		

-amed

-amed		-aimed
ashamed	named	aimed
blamed	tamed	claimed
famed	unashamed	exclaimed
framed	unnamed	proclaimed
inflamed	untamed	unclaimed

-ammer

-ammer	-amour	-ammar
hammer	clamour	grammar
programmer	glamour	
stammer		

-amp

-amp			
amp	clamp	lamp	stamp
camp	cramp	ramp	tramp
champ	damp	scamp	

15

-amper

-amper

camper	hamper	scamper
damper	pamper	tamper

-an

-an

an	fan	Peter Pan	than
ban	flash in the	plan	van
Batman	pan	ran	weatherman
began	frying pan	scan	
bogeyman	gran	signalman	-anne
bran	handyman	snowman	Anne
businessman	Isle of Man	span	Joanne
cameraman	Japan	spick-and-	Leanne
can	man	span	
caravan	man-to-man	Spiderman	-ann
clan	orang-utan	Superman	Ann
Dan	pan	tan	

-ance

-ance

advance	France	trance
chance	glance	
dance	lance	
entrance (= to charm)	prance	

-ancing

-ancing

advancing	entrancing	prancing
dancing	glancing	

-and

-and

			-anned
armband	hand	sand	banned
and	land	second-hand	canned
band	Lapland	stand	planned
bland	left hand	strand	scanned
brand	lend a hand	underhand	tanned
close at hand	misunderstand	understand	unplanned
Disneyland	near at hand	Wonderland	
expand	offhand		
grand	right hand		

-anda

-anda	-ander	
Amanda	bystander	
panda	gander	Goosey goosey *gander*
veranda	grander	Where's the **veranda**
		Upstairs or downstairs
	-andah	And can I take my **panda**?
	verandah	

-ander¹

Like the sound in the word gander – look up -anda for words ending in this sound

-ander²

Like the sound in the word wander – look up -onder for words ending in this sound

-anding

-anding

expanding
landing

misunder-
standing

outstanding
standing

understanding

-andy

-andy

Andy
brandy

candy
dandy

handy
Mandy

Sandy
sandy

-ane

Look up -ain for words ending in this sound

-ang

-ang

bang
boomerang
clang
fang
gang

go with a
 bang
hang
orang-outang
pang

rang
sang
slang
sprang
twang

-ingue
meringue

-ange

-ange

arrange
change

exchange
free-range

range
rearrange

strange

-anger¹

-anger

anger
banger

clanger
cliffhanger

hanger

-angar
hangar

-anger²

-anger

arranger	Hermione	ranger
danger	Granger	stranger
endanger	manger	

-angle

-angle

angle	jangle	strangle	wangle
bangle	mangle	tangle	
dangle	rectangle	triangle	

-ank

-ank

bank	frank	spank
blank	gangplank	stank
clank	plank	swank
crank	prank	tank
dank	rank	thank
drank	sank	
Frank	shrank	

A child should not be judged by
The way they play a **prank**,
An adult should not be judged by
Their money in the **bank**.

-anner

-anner	-anna	-ana	-annah
banner	Anna	bandana	Hannah
manner	bandanna	Diana	
planner	Joanna		-anor
scanner			manor
spanner			

-ant

-ant		-an't	-aren't
chant	plant	can't	aren't
elephant	slant	shan't	
enchant	transplant		-aunt
grant			aunt

-ap

-ap			
booby-trap	handicap	put on your	tap
cap	lap	thinking cap	trap
chap	madcap	rap	unwrap
clap	map	sap	wrap
feather in your	mousetrap	scrap	yap
cap	nap	slap	zap
flap	overlap	snap	
gap		strap	

-ape

-ape			
ape	gape	landscape	scrape
cape	grape	measuring tape	Sellotape®
drape	in shape	out of shape	shape
escape	jape	reshape	tape

-aper

-aper

blotting paper	scraper	wastepaper	
caper	skyscraper	wrapping	
newspaper	taper	paper	
notepaper	toilet paper	writing paper	
paper	tracing paper		
sandpaper	wallpaper		

-apour

vapour

-aph

-aph	-aff	-arf
autograph	staff	scarf
graph		
paragraph	-affe	-augh
photograph	giraffe	laugh

-alf

behalf
calf
half

Hey superstar, yes you giraffe, Can I have your autograph?

-aps

-aps

booby-traps	maps	slaps	zaps
caps	mousetraps	snaps	
chaps	naps	straps	**-apse**
claps	overlaps	taps	apse
flaps	perhaps	traps	collapse
gaps	raps	unwraps	lapse
handicaps	saps	wraps	
laps	scraps	yaps	

21

-ar

-ar			-aar
afar	spar	pa	bazaar
bar	star	spa	
car	superstar	ta	-ah
caviar	tar	ta-ta	hurrah
char			
cigar	-a	-are	-arre
far	bra	are	bizarre
guitar	grandma	caviare	
jar	grandpa		
motorcar	la-la	-aa	
scar	ma	baa	

-ard

-ard		-arred
backyard	postcard	barred
bard	regard	charred
barnyard	safeguard	scarred
bodyguard	scratchcard	starred
bombard	yard	
card		
coastguard		
farmyard		
guard		
hard		
lard		
leotard		
placard		

-are

-are	-air	-ear	-eir
aware	affair	bear	heir
bare	air	pear	their
beware	armchair	swear	
blare	chair	tear (= to rip)	-ayer
care	deckchair	teddy bear	prayer
Clare	despair	underwear	
compare	eclair	wear	-ayor
dare	fair		mayor
declare	flair	-ere	
flare	funfair	anywhere	-er
glare	hair	everywhere	Cher
hardware	lair	somewhere	
hare	midair	there	-ey're
mare	open-air	where	they're
prepare	pair		
rare	repair	-aire	
scare	rocking chair	Claire	
share	stair	millionaire	
snare	Tony Blair	questionnaire	
software	unfair		
spare			
square			
stare			
unaware			

-arge

-arge	
barge	in charge
charge	large
discharge	Marge
enlarge	

-aring

-aring
blaring	raring
caring	scaring
comparing	sharing
daring	sparing
declaring	staring
glaring	uncaring
preparing	

-earing
bearing
hard-wearing
tearing
swearing
wearing

-airing
airing
despairing
pairing
repairing

-arity

-arity
charity	hilarity	regularity
clarity	peculiarity	similarity
familiarity	popularity	vulgarity

-ark

-ark
ark	Jurassic Park	shark
bark	landmark	shot in the dark
Central Park	lark	spark
dark	Mark	stark
Denmark	mark	theme park
Hyde Park	park	trademark
in the dark	remark	

-aq
Iraq

-erk
clerk

-arn

-arn
barn
darn
spin a yarn
yarn

-an
Afghanistan
Iran
Koran
Pakistan

24

-arry		-arrie	-ary
Barry	Larry	Carrie	Gary
carry	marry		
Garry	remarry		
Harry	starry		

-art		-eart	
apart	part	change of heart	heart-to-heart
art	smart	heart	lose your heart
Bart	start		young at heart
cart	tart		
chart			
dart			
depart			
jam tart			

Garry was quite **smart**
He sure knew how to barter,
But Carrie stole his **heart**,
That means Carrie was smarter.

-arter		
barter	garter	starter
charter	smarter	

-ary		-airy
canary	vary	airy
contrary (= obstinate and awkward)	wary	dairy
		fairy
Mary		hairy
scary		

-ase

Like the sound in the word case – look up -ace for words ending in this sound

-aser

-aser	-aiser	-azer	-azor
eraser	fund-raiser	blazer	razor
laser			

-ash

-ash

ash	gash	quick as a flash	thrash
bash	gnash		trash
cash	hash	rash	
clash	have a bash	sash	-ache
crash	lash	slapdash	moustache
dash	mash	slash	
flash	nappy rash	splash	

-ass¹

-ass		-as
ass	lass	alas
bass (= a fish)	mass	gas

-ass²

-ass			-arse
brass	grass	snake in the grass	sparse
class	pass	stained glass	
first-class	second-class		
glass			

-ast

-ast			-assed
Belfast	fast	too good to	passed
blast	last	last	
cast	mast	vast	
contrast	past		

-aste

Look up -aced for words ending in this sound

-aster

-aster			-astor
broadcaster	master	schoolmaster	pastor
disaster	newscaster		
faster	plaster		
headmaster	ringmaster		

-astic

-astic	
drastic	sarcastic
elastic	plastic
enthusiastic	unenthusiastic
fantastic	
gymnastic	
over-enthusiastic	

*A schoolteacher made out of **plastic**
Was quite flexible and **gymnastic**,
He could twist through the air
And land straight on a chair,
All the kids thought his feet were **fantastic**.*

-at

-atch

-ate

-ate			-ait
appreciate	fate	second-rate	bait
ate	first-rate	separate (= to part)	wait
calculate	gate		
candidate	grate	skate	-aight
celebrate	hate	slate	straight
classmate	hesitate	state	
concentrate	ice-skate	third-rate	-eat
confiscate	imitate	translate	great
congratulate	in-line skate	up-to-date	
cooperate	irritate	update	
crate	Kate	vibrate	
create	late		
date	mate	-eight	
debate	numberplate	eight	
decorate	operate	heavyweight	
estate	out-of-date	lightweight	
estimate (= to guess)	plate	overweight	
	rate	weight	
exaggerate	roller-skate		

-ated

-ated			-aited
belated	exaggerated	outdated	waited
calculated	frustrated	related	
celebrated	gold-plated	separated	
complicated	grated	stated	
concentrated	hated	translated	
confiscated	hesitated	updated	
created	imitated		
dated	irritated		
decorated	isolated		
educated	operated		

-ater[1]

-ater	-aughter	-orter	-arter
backwater	daughter	porter	quarter
freshwater	goddaughter	reporter	
in hot water	granddaughter	shorter	-ortar
rainwater	great-	supporter	mortar
saltwater	granddaughter		
underwater	slaughter		
water	stepdaughter		

-ater[2]

Like the sound in the word skater – look up -ator for words ending in this sound

-ath

-ath		-earth
Bath	footpath	hearth
bath	path	
bubble bath	warpath	

-ather

-ather	-arther
father	farther
godfather	
grandfather	
great-	
grandfather	
lather	
rather	
stepfather	

-ating

-ating			-aiting
celebrating	frustrating	operating	waiting
concentrating	grating	roller-skating	
creating	hating	separating	-eighting
dating	hesitating	skating	weighting
decorating	ice-skating	translating	
exaggerating	in-line skating		
fascinating	irritating		

-ation

-ation			vaccination
abbreviation	exclamation	population	vibration
association	explanation	preparation	
calculation	generation	presentation	
carnation	hesitation	pronunciation	-atian
celebration	illustration	punctuation	Alsatian
combination	imagination	regulation	Dalmatian
concentration	imitation	relation	
conversation	information	relaxation	
cooperation	invitation	reputation	
creation	irritation	sensation	
decoration	multiplication	separation	
dedication	nation	situation	
demonstration	observation	starvation	
education	occupation	station	
exaggeration	operation	temptation	
examination	organization	translation	

The mind is more than just a place to store
   your **information**,
The mind is more, it is the base of your
   imagination.

-ator

-ator	-ater	-aighter	-ata
alligator	cater	straighter	data
calculator	crater		
commentator	grater	-aiter	-eater
creator	hater	waiter	greater
decorator	ice-skater		
demonstrator	later	-aitor	
equator	skater	traitor	
escalator			
gladiator			
illustrator			
operator			
radiator			
spectator			

-atter

-atter			
batter	flatter	matter	shatter
chatter	latter	natter	splatter
clatter	mad as a	patter	
fatter	hatter	scatter	

-atty

-atty		
batty	fatty	scatty
catty	Patty	tatty
chatty	ratty	

-aughter

Look up -ater[1] for words ending in this sound

-ault

-ault		-alt
assault	somersault	malt
fault	vault	salt

-aunt

-aunt		
flaunt	haunt	taunt
gaunt	jaunt	

-ave

-ave			
aftershave	Dave	microwave	slave
behave	engrave	misbehave	wave
brave	forgave	rave	
cave	gave	save	-ey've
crave	grave	shave	they've

-aver

-aver			-avour
braver	raver	waver	do me a favour
life-saver	saver		favour
quaver	shaver		flavour

-aving

-aving			
behaving	life-saving	saving	waving
engraving	misbehaving	shaving	
face-saving	raving	time-saving	

-aw

Look up -ore for words ending in this sound

-awl

Look up -all for words ending in this sound

-awn

Look up -orn for words ending in this sound

-aws

-aws	-oors	-ours	-auze
claws	doors	fours	gauze
draws	floors	on all fours	
flaws	indoors	pours	-awers
Jaws	outdoors	yours	drawers
jaws	out-of-doors		
laws			
paws	-ause	-aus	
saws	applause	Santa Claus	
thaws	cause		
	clause		
-ores	pause		
bores			
chores	-oars		
cores	boars		
explores	oars		
pores	roars		
scores	soars		
shores			
stores			

-ay

-ay		-ey	-eigh
anyway	play	convey	neigh
ashtray	portray	disobey	sleigh
away	pray	grey	weigh
bay	present-day	hey	
betray	railway	obey	-et
castaway	ray	prey	bouquet
child's play	relay	survey	buffet (= a
clay	repay	they	selection of
day	replay		food)
day-to-day	runaway	-A	cabaret
decay	say	AA	
delay	spray	FA (= Football	-K
dismay	stay	Association)	OK
display	straightaway	LA	UK
everyday	stray	RSPCA	
faraway	sway	USA	
gay	takeaway	YMCA	
giveaway	tearaway		
halfway	today		
hay	tray		
highway	way		
hooray	wordplay		
lay	yesterday		
May			
may			
midday			
motorway			
out-of-the-way			
passageway			
pay			

*If a high way's
Not a highway
Could it be a motorway?
And if I take away
A bend today
Would it be a straightaway?*

-ayed

Look up -ade for words ending in this sound

-ayer

-ayer

betrayer
bricklayer

layer
payer

player

-eyer

greyer

-aying

-aying

betraying
decaying
delaying
displaying
laying
paying
playing
portraying

praying
repaying
replaying
saying
spraying
staying
swaying

-eying

conveying
disobeying
greying
obeying
preying
surveying

-eighing

neighing
weighing

-ays

-ays		-aze	-aise
ashtrays	rays	amaze	mayonnaise
bays	relays	blaze	praise
betrays	repays	craze	raise
castaways	replays	daze	
days	runaways	gaze	-eighs
delays	says	graze	neighs
displays	sprays	haze	sleighs
highways	strays	laze	weighs
lays	sways	maze	
motorways	takeaways		-ase
nowadays	tearaways	-eys	catchphrase
passageways	trays	conveys	phrase
pays	ways	disobeys	
plays		obeys	-aize
portrays		preys	maize
prays		surveys	
railways			

-azed

-azed		-aised
amazed	glazed	praised
blazed	grazed	raised
dazed	lazed	
gazed		

-azing

-azing		-aising
amazing	glazing	hair-raising
blazing	grazing	praising
gazing		raising

-each

-each

			-eech
beach	peach	teach	beech
bleach	preach		leech
each	reach		screech
			speech

-ead[1]

Like the sound in the word head – look up -ed for words ending in this sound

-ead[2]

Like the sound in the word bead – look up -eed for words ending in this sound

-eaded

-eaded

beheaded	dreaded	headed	unleaded
bigheaded	empty-headed	light-headed	

-eader

-eader		-eeder	-edar
cheerleader	newsreader	breeder	cedar
leader	reader	feeder	
mind-reader	ringleader		

-eady

-eady		-eddie	-eddy
already	steady	Eddie	teddy
ready	unsteady	Freddie	

-eak

-eak	-eek	-ique	-ic
beak	cheek	antique	chic
bleak	geek	boutique	
creak	Greek	physique	-iek
freak	hide-and-seek	technique	shriek
leak	leek	unique	
peak	meek		-ikh
sneak	midweek		Sikh
speak	peek		
squeak	reek		
streak	seek		
tweak	sleek		
weak	week		

The **freak** of the **week** was a **leek**
With a cheeky and squeaky **physique**.
It really was freaky
And creaky and leaky,
Believe me
This **geek** was **unique**.

-eaker

-eaker		-eeker
beaker	speaker	meeker
bleaker	streaker	seeker
loudspeaker	weaker	sleeker
sneaker		

-eaky

-eaky		-eeky
creaky	squeaky	cheeky
freaky	streaky	geeky
leaky		
peaky		
sneaky		

-eal

-eal

			-e'll
appeal	seal	ferris wheel	he'll
big deal	squeal	genteel	she'll
conceal	steal	heel	we'll
congeal	veal	keel	
deal	zeal	kneel	-eil
heal		peel	Neil
meal	-eel	reel	
ordeal	cartwheel	stainless steel	
peal	eel	steel	
reveal	feel	wheel	

-ealed

-ealed	-eeled	-ield
appealed	cartwheeled	afield
concealed	flat-heeled	battlefield
congealed	four-wheeled	field
healed	high-heeled	midfield
pealed	low-heeled	shield
revealed	peeled	wield
sealed	three-wheeled	yield
squealed	two-wheeled	
unconcealed	well-heeled	

-ealer

-ealer	-eeler
concealer	feeler
dealer	potato peeler
faith healer	three-wheeler
healer	
squealer	

-ealing

-ealing		-eeling	-eiling
appealing	revealing	feeling	ceiling
concealing	sealing	kneeling	
congealing	squealing	peeling	
dealing	stealing	reeling	
double-	unappealing	unfeeling	
dealing	wheeling and		
faith healing	dealing		
healing			
pealing			

-eam

-eam		-eem	-eme
beam	scream	deem	blaspheme
bream	seam	esteem	extreme
clotted cream	sour cream	redeem	scheme
cream	steam	seem	supreme
daydream	stream	self-esteem	theme
downstream	team	teem	
dream	upstream		-ime
gleam	whipped		regime
ice-cream	cream		
let off steam			
mainstream			
midstream			
ream			

-ean

Look up -een for words ending in this sound

-eaning

-eaning
cleaning
dry-cleaning
leaning
meaning

spring-
cleaning
well-meaning

-eening
preening
screening

-ining
trampolining

-eap

Look up -eep for words ending in this sound

-ear¹

Like the sound in the word bear – look up -are for words ending in this sound

-ear²

-ear
appear
clear
dear
disappear
ear
fear
gear
hear
near
nuclear
overhear
rear
smear
spear
tear (= a drop
of water)

unclear
year

-eer
beer
career
cheer
deer
engineer
jeer
mountaineer
peer
queer
reindeer
sheer
sneer

steer
veer
volunteer

-ere
atmosphere
here
insincere
interfere
mere
persevere
severe
sincere
sphere

-ier
pier
tier

-eare
Shakespeare

-e're
we're

-ir
souvenir

-earch

-earch	-urch	-erch	-irch
research	church	perch	birch
search	lurch		

-earer

-earer	-arer	-airer	-arah
bearer	carer	fairer	Sarah
wearer	rarer		

		-ara	
		Sara	

-earing

-earing	-eering	-earring	-ering
appearing	cheering	earring	interfering
clearing	engineering		
disappearing	jeering		
endearing	mountaineer- ing		
fearing	sneering		
hearing	steering		
searing			

-earth

-earth	-irth
down-to-earth	birth
earth	
	-orth
-erth	worth
berth	

Priceless

You should know what this planet's **worth**
If your place of **birth** is **earth**.

-easant

-easant	-esent
peasant	present
pheasant	(= here or
pleasant	= a gift)
unpleasant	

-ease¹

-ease	-iece	-ice	-ese
cease	mantelpiece	Nice	obese
crease	masterpiece	police	
decease	niece		-ys
decrease	piece	-eace	Rhys
grease		peace	
increase	-eece		
lease	fleece	-eese	
release	Greece	geese	

-ease²

Like the sound in the word please – look up **-ees** for words ending in this sound

-eased¹

-eased	-east	-iest
ceased	beast	priest
creased	east	
deceased	feast	
decreased	least	
greased	yeast	
increased		
leased		
released		

-eased²

-eased		-eezed	-eized
diseased	pleased	sneezed	seized
displeased	teased	squeezed	
eased		wheezed	

-easing¹

-easing		-eecing	-iecing
ceasing	increasing	fleecing	piecing
creasing	leasing		
decreasing	releasing	-icing	
greasing	unceasing	policing	

-easing²

-easing		-eezing	
displeasing	pleasing	freezing	squeezing
easing	teasing	sneezing	wheezing

-east

Look up -eased¹ for words ending in this sound

-easure

-easure		-eisure
measure	treasure	leisure
pleasure		

-easy

-easy		-eezy
easy	uneasy	breezy
queasy		sneezy

-eat

-eat	-eet	-ete	-eit
beat	discreet	athlete	conceit
bleat	Downing	compete	deceit
cheat	Street	complete	
defeat	feet	delete	-eipt
eat	fleet	incomplete	receipt
feat	greet	obsolete	
heartbeat	indiscreet	secrete	
heat	meet		
meat	sheet	-ite	
neat	sleet	elite	
peat	street	petite	
pleat	sweet	suite	
repeat	the patter of		
retreat	tiny feet		
seat	tweet		
treat	white as a		
wheat	sheet		

-eaten

-eaten	-eeten	-eton
beaten	sweeten	Eton
eaten		
moth-eaten		
neaten		
unbeaten		
uneaten		
weatherbeaten		

-eater

-eater	-itre	-eeter	-ita
anteater	centilitre	sweeter	Gita
beater	litre	teeter	Rita
eater	millilitre		
heater		-eter	-eetah
man-eater		meter	cheetah
neater		Peter	
world-beater			

-etre
centimetre
kilometre
metre
millimetre

Peter met Gita one day at the gym,
Gita said, 'Peter, let's go for a swim'.
Peter said, 'Gita, I can't swim, let's talk'.
'Okay', said Gita, 'let's go for a walk'.

-eath¹

-eath		-eeth
beneath	underneath	teeth
heath	wreath	
sheath		

-eath²

-eath		-eth	
breath	hang on like	Beth	Nazareth
death	grim death	Elizabeth	
	out of breath		

-eathe

-eathe	-eethe
breathe	seethe
sheathe	teethe
unsheathe	

-eather

Like the sound in the word weather – look up -ether for words
ending in this sound

-eating

-eating			-eeting
beating	eating	retreating	fleeting
bleating	heating	seating	greeting
cheating	man-eating	treating	meeting
defeating	repeating		sleeting

-eck

-eck			-ech
check	pain in the	V-neck	high-tech
deck	neck	wreck	
double-check	peck		-eque
fleck	polo neck	-ek	cheque
neck	speck	Shrek	
nervous wreck	up to your	trek	
	neck		

-ecks

-ecks		-ex	-ecs
Becks	specks	complex	specs
checks	V-necks	ex	
double-checks	wrecks	flex	-eks
flecks		multiplex	treks
necks		perplex	
pecks		vex	-exe
polo necks			annexe

-ect

-ect			-ecked
affect	inject	reflect	checked
after-effect	inspect	reject	flecked
architect	neglect	respect	henpecked
collect	object	select	pecked
connect	perfect	self-respect	shipwrecked
correct	prefect	subject	unchecked
defect	project	suspect	wrecked
detect	protect		
direct			
effect			
elect			
expect			
incorrect			
indirect			
infect			

My sister is a **prefect**
My sister thinks she's **perfect**,
She thinks she is a teacher in disguise,
But she's never read the classics
And she's bad at mathematics,
And she never talks to me and I'm so wise.

-ected

-ected	
affected	rejected
collected	respected
connected	selected
directed	suspected
expected	unexpected
infected	unprotected
inspected	
neglected	
objected	
protected	

-ection

-ection

affection	inspection
collection	objection
connection	perfection
correction	protection
cross-section	reflection
direction	rejection
election	section
infection	selection
injection	

-exion

complexion

-ective

-ective

collective	protective
detective	reflective
effective	selective
objective	

-ector

-ector

collector	protector
director	sector
film director	selector
Hector	stamp
inspector	collector
lie detector	
projector	

-ectar

nectar

-ed

-edge

-ee

Look up -y¹ for words ending in this sound

-eed

-eed		-ead	-ede
agreed	seed	bead	centipede
bleed	speed	knead	millipede
breed	succeed	lead (= to	stampede
deed	tweed	guide)	Swede
disagreed	weak-	mislead	
exceed	kneed	plead	-e'd
feed	weed	read	he'd
freed			she'd
greed			we'd
guaranteed			
heed			-eid
high-speed			Eid
indeed			
knock-kneed			
need			
proceed			
reed			
seaweed			

Jet-propelled
All were **agreed**,
Once expelled
It moved at **speed**.

-eedier

-eedier	-edia	-aedia
greedier	encyclopedia	encyclopaedia
needier	media	
seedier	multimedia	
speedier		
weedier		

-eeding

-eeding		-eading	-eding
bleeding	speeding	beading	preceding
breeding	succeeding	kneading	stampeding
exceeding	weeding	leading	
feeding		misleading	
needing		pleading	
proceeding		reading	

-eedy

-eedy			-eady
greedy	seedy	weedy	beady
needy	speedy		

-eef

Look up -ief for words ending in this sound

-eeing

-eeing		-eing	-iing
agreeing	refereeing	being	skiing
disagreeing	seeing	wellbeing	water-skiing
fleeing	sightseeing		
freeing			-eying
			keying

-eek

Look up -eak for words ending in this sound

-eel

Look up -eal for words ending in this sound

-een

-een	-ine	-ean	-ene
Aberdeen	answering machine	bean	gene
been	aubergine	butter bean	polythene
between	knitting machine	clean	scene
big screen	limousine machine	Dean	serene
canteen	magazine	dry-clean	
eighteen	margarine	jellybean	-e'en
evergreen	marine	kidney bean	Hallowe'en
fifteen	nectarine	lean	
fourteen	ravine	mean	-ein
go-between	routine	Mr Bean	protein
green	sardine	runner bean	
Halloween	sewing machine	soya bean	-eine
has-been	submarine	spring-clean	caffeine
in-between	tambourine	unclean	
keen	tangerine		
nineteen	time machine		
preen	trampoline		
queen	washing machine		
screen			
seen			
seventeen			
sheen			
sixteen			
spleen			
teen			
thirteen			
umpteen			
unforeseen			
unseen			
widescreen			
windscreen			

I'll buy that wicked **time machine**
When time has passed
And I'm **eighteen**.

-eep

-eep

asleep	seep
beep	sheep
bleep	sleep
creep	steep
deep	sweep
Jeep®	upkeep
keep	weep
knee-deep	
peep	

-eap

cheap	leap
dirt-cheap	reap
heap	scrapheap

> I'm so busy counting **sheep**
> That I just don't have time to **sleep**.

-eeper

-eeper

beeper	doorkeeper	steeper
bleeper	gamekeeper	sweeper
bookkeeper	goalkeeper	timekeeper
carpet-sweeper	housekeeper	wicketkeeper
creeper	keeper	
deeper	shopkeeper	
	sleeper	

-eaper

cheaper
reaper

-eeping

-eeping

beeping	housekeeping	sleeping
bookkeeping	keeping	sweeping
creeping	peacekeeping	timekeeping
goalkeeping	safe-keeping	weeping

-eaping

heaping
leaping
reaping

-eer

Look up -ear² for words ending in this sound

-ees

-ees	-eeze	-ese	-ise
agrees	antifreeze	Chinese	expertise
bees	breeze	Japanese	Louise
chimpanzees	deep-freeze	Pekinese	
degrees	freeze	Portuguese	-eaze
disagrees	sneeze	these	sleaze
dungarees	squeeze		
fees	wheeze	-eas	-eize
frees		overseas	seize
guarantees	-ease	peas	
knees	disease	seas	-es
referees	displease		recipes
refugees	ease	-eese	
sees	please	cheese	-eys
threes	tease	like chalk and	keys
trees		cheese	
			-eze
		-e's	trapeze
		he's	
		she's	

-eet

Look up -eat for words ending in this sound

-eeze

Look up -ees for words ending in this sound

-eg

-eg

an arm and a
 leg
beg
break a leg
keg

leg
peg

-egg

Easter egg
egg
nest egg

-eive

Look up -ieve for words ending in this sound

-ell

-ell

bell
cell
dwell
farewell
fell
hell
seashell
sell
shell
smell
spell
swell

tell
Tinkerbell
tortoiseshell
unwell
well
yell

-el

caramel
carousel
compel
decibel
excel
expel
gel
hotel
lapel
Manuel
motel
parallel

personnel
propel

-elle

belle
Danielle
gazelle
Michelle

-elled

-elled

compelled
excelled
expelled
gelled

jet-propelled
propelled
smelled
spelled

swelled
yelled

-eld

held
weld
withheld

-eller

-eller
bestseller	seller		
bookseller	speller		
dweller	storyteller		
fortune-teller			
propeller			

-ella
Cinderella
umbrella

-ellar
cellar

-ela
Nelson
Mandela

-elling

-elling

bestselling	expelling	smelling	swelling
compelling	selling	spelling	telling
dwelling	shelling	sweet-smelling	yelling

-ellow

-ellow

bellow	mellow	cello
fellow	yellow	

-ello

-elly

-elly

belly	jelly	Nelly	telly
Ellie	Kelly	smelly	welly

-elt

-elt

belt	heartfelt	pelt	dealt
dwelt	knelt	smelt	
felt	melt	spelt	

-ealt

-em

-em	-m	-egm	-emn
Bethlehem	a.m.	phlegm	condemn
gem	p.m.		
hem			
Jerusalem			
stem			
them			

-ember

-ember	
December	November
member	remember
non-member	September

-empt

-empt

attempt
contempt
exempt
tempt

-en

-en		-ain
amen	men	again
Ben	pen	once again
den	pigpen	
fen	playpen	
glen	ten	
Gwen	then	
hen	when	
Ken	wren	

-ence

-ence

		-ense	
commence	self-defence	dense	intense
defence	violence	expense	sense
disobedience		frankincense	suspense
evidence		immense	tense
excellence		incense	
fence			
innocence			
obedience			
offence			
pretence			
residence			

The world needs love and peace
*It's simple, it makes **sense**,*
The fighting has to cease
*Let's end the **violence**.*

-ench

-ench

bench	drench	quench	trench
clench	French	stench	

-end

-end

			-iend
at a loose end	make some-one's hair stand on end	suspend	befriend
attend	mend	tend	friend
bend	offend	to the very end	
blend	on the mend	to the bitter end	
contend	pretend	trend	
defend	recommend	weekend	
depend	round the bend		
end	send		
extend	spend		
intend			
lend			

-endant

-endant	-endent
attendant	dependent (= someone who depends on another)
defendant	
dependant (= depending on a person)	
pendant	independent
	superintendent

-ender

-ender			-enda
blender	moneylender	spender	agenda
contender	offender	surrender	Brenda
defender	pretender	tender	Glenda
fender	render		
gender	sender		-endour
lender	slender		splendour

-ending

-ending			
attending	ending	never-ending	tending
bending	extending	offending	
blending	intending	pretending	-iending
defending	lending	sending	befriending
depending	mending	spending	

-enny

-enny		-any
a pretty penny	penny	any
Jenny	spend a penny	many
Kenny		
Penny		

-ense

Look up -ence for words ending in this sound

-ent

-ent

accent	environment	measurement	segment
accident	event	monument	sent
advertisement	excellent	ornament	spent
argument	fragment	parliament	tent
astonishment	frequent	per cent	torment
bent	incident	present	tournament
cement	innocent	prevent	went
consent	instrument	punishment	
content	intelligent	regiment	-eant
dent	invent	relent	leant
development	Kent	rent	meant
document	Lent	represent	
element	lent	resent	
embarrassment	magnificent	scent	

-ental

-ental		-entil	-entle
accidental	mental	lentil	gentle
dental	rental		
environmental	sentimental		

-enter

-enter	-entor	-entre
enter	inventor	centre
presenter	tormentor	
re-enter		

-ention

-ention
attention
detention
intention
invention
mention
prevention

-ension
extension
pension
suspension
tension

Dear teacher,
Did I **mention**
That I don't like **detention**?

-ep

-ep
prep
rep
step

-epp
Johnny Depp

-ept

-ept
accept
crept
except
kept
overslept

slept
swept
wept

-eapt
leapt

-epped
stepped

-er

Look up **-ur** for words ending in this sound

-erb

-erb		-urb
adverb	superb	curb
herb	verb	disturb
kerb		perturb

-erge

-erge	-urge	-ourge
emerge	purge	scourge
merge	surge	
verge	urge	

-erior

-erior	-earier	-eerier	-eria
exterior	drearier	cheerier	bacteria
inferior	wearier	eerier	cafeteria
interior			
superior			

-erry

-erry			-ery
berry	Kerry	sherry	very
cherry	Londonderry	Terry	
Derry	make merry		-ury
ferry	merry		bury

-erse

-erse	-urse	-earse	-orse
diverse	curse	hearse	worse
immerse	nurse	rehearse	
reverse	purse		
universe			
verse			

-ersion

-ersion	-ertion	-ursion
conversion	desertion	excursion
diversion	exertion	
version	insertion	

-ert

Look up -irt for words ending in this sound

-erve

-erve		-urve
conserve	serve	curve
deserve	swerve	
nerve		
observe		
preserve		
reserve		

When folk get old I do observe
They get the face that they deserve.

-ese

Look up -ees for words ending in this sound

-esh

-esh
flesh
fresh
mesh
refresh

-ess

-ess			-s
address	impress	undress	HMS
bless	laziness	unless	NHS
chess	less	untidiness	PS
colourless	Loch Ness	wickedness	SAS
confess	mess	wilderness	SOS
couldn't-care-less	nastiness		US
cress	nevertheless		VHS
depress	penniless		
distress	possess		-es
dress	press		yes
eagerness	princess		
excess	progress		
express	silliness		
gentleness	stress		
guess	success		
	tactless		

-essed

Look up -est for words ending in this sound

-esser

-esser	-essor	-essa
dresser	professor	Vanessa
hairdresser	successor	
lesser	word processor	

-essing

-essing

blessing	dressing	impressing	progressing
confessing	expressing	messing	undressing
depressing	guessing	possessing	word
distressing	hairdressing	pressing	processing

-ession

-ession

			-eshen
confession	impression	procession	freshen
depression	obsession	profession	
expression	possession	session	

-essive

-essive

aggressive	impressive	possessive

-est

-est		-essed	-east
arrest	protest	addressed	abreast
best	quest	blessed	
chest	request	confessed	
conquest	rest	depressed	
contest	second-best	distressed	
crest	suggest	dressed	
detest	test	expressed	
digest	vest	guessed	
guest	west	impressed	
jest	zest	stressed	
nest		undressed	
pest		well-dressed	

-ester

-ester

Chester
fester
jester
Leicester

Manchester
pester
protester
Sylvester

tester

-estor

investor

-et

-et

alphabet
bet
cadet
clarinet
duet
forget
fret
get
Internet
jet
let
met
net
pet
quartet
regret
Romeo and
 Juliet
set

upset
vet
wet
yet

-ette

brunette
cassette
cigarette
courgette
launderette
majorette
pirouette
serviette
silhouette

-eat

sweat
threat

-ebt

debt

Romeo and Juliet
Did not meet on the Internet.

-etch

-etch

fetch
sketch

stretch
wretch

-eth

Look up -eath[2] for words ending in this sound

-ether

-ether		-eather	
altogether	together	feather	under the
at the end of	whether	heather	weather
your tether		leather	weather
get-together			

-etic

-etic

athletic	energetic	poetic
cosmetic	magnetic	sympathetic
diabetic	pathetic	synthetic

-ette

Look up -et for words ending in this sound

-etter

-etter	-eater	-etta
better	sweater	Viennetta®
go-getter		
jetsetter		
letter		
newsletter		
setter		
trendsetter		
wetter		

-etting

-etting			-eating
betting	jetsetting	regretting	sweating
forgetting	jetting	setting	
fretting	letting	upsetting	
getting	netting	wetting	

-ettle

-ettle		-etal
kettle	settle	metal
nettle	unsettle	petal

-ever

-ever		-evor
clever	whenever	Trevor
ever	wherever	
forever	whoever	
however		
never		
whatever		
whatsoever		

Sometimes my brother **Trevor**
Makes no sense **whatsoever**,
He's sweet and cute
However,
He's really not that **clever**.

-ew

-ew			
Andrew	crew	knew	screw
askew	dew	Matthew	shrew
bird's-eye view	drew	mew	stew
blew	few	new	strew
brand-new	flew	pew	threw
brew	grew	phew	view
cashew	interview	renew	withdrew
chew	Jew	review	yew

-ue
avenue
barbecue
black-and-blue
blue
clue
cue
due
glue
overdue
pursue
subdue
Sue
sue
true
undue
untrue

-o
ado
do
lasso
outdo
overdo
redo
talking-to
to
to-do
undo
well-to-do
who
you-know-who

-oo
ballyhoo
bamboo
boo
cockatoo
coo
hullabaloo
kangaroo
shampoo
tattoo
too
zoo

-u
flu
Hindu
IOU

-oe
canoe
shoe

-ou
thank you
you

-eue
queue

-ewe
ewe

-ough
through

-Q
IQ

-wo
two

A new **kangaroo** known as *Sue*
Was happy to **chew** on *bamboo*,
So this confused minor
Migrated to China
Where she lives up a tree with a ***view***.

-ewer

-ewer	-uer	-oer
brewer	bluer	wrongdoer
fewer	pursuer	
interviewer	truer	
newer		
reviewer		
sewer (= a drain)		
skewer		
viewer		

-ex

Look up -ecks for words ending in this sound

-ey

Look up -ay for words ending in this sound

-ial

-ial	
denial	sundial
dial	trial
redial	

-ib

-ib	
ad-lib	jib
bib	nib
crib	rib
fib	
glib	

-ibe

-ibe
bribe
describe
inscribe
prescribe
tribe

-ic

Look up -ick for words ending in this sound

-ice

-ice
advice
device
dice
entice
ice
lice
mice
nice
price
rice
sacrifice
slice

spice
suffice
trice
twice
vice

-ise
concise
paradise
precise

-icious

-icious
delicious
malicious
suspicious
vicious

-itious
ambitious
superstitious

-ick

-icked

-icken

-icker

-icker

bicker	slicker
flicker	sticker
nit-picker	thicker
picnicker	wicker
quicker	
sicker	

-icar

vicar

-icket

-icket

cricket	ticket
picket	wicket
thicket	

-ickle

-ickle

fickle	tickle
pickle	trickle
prickle	

-ickly

-ickly

prickly	sickly	thickly
quickly	slickly	

-ickness

-ickness

homesickness	seasickness	slickness	travel-sickness
quickness	sickness	thickness	

-icks	-ics	-ix
bricks	acrobatics	crucifix
candlesticks	antics	fix
chicks	classics	mix
clicks	dramatics	six
fiddlesticks	electronics	
flicks	lunatics	
kicks	mathematics	
licks	mechanics	
like a ton of	physics	
bricks	politics	
limericks		
picks		
pricks		
sticks		
ticks		
tricks		
wicks		

*Normally I get my **kicks** writing silly **limericks**,*
Sometimes I change my style,
That's being versatile.

-icky

-icky	-ickie	-ickey	-ikki
Nicky	brickie	Mickey	Nikki
picky	sickie		
Ricky		-icki	
sticky		Vicki	
tricky			

-ics

Look up -icks for words ending in this sound

-ict

Look up -icked for words ending in this sound

-iction

-iction

		-ixion
addiction	non-fiction	crucifixion
contradiction	prediction	
conviction	restriction	
eviction		
fiction		
friction		

-id

-id

bid	kid	quid
did	lid	rid
forbid	Madrid	skid
grid	mid	slid
hid	pyramid	squid

-idal

-idal	**-idle**	**-idol**
bridal	bridle	idol
suicidal	idle	
tidal	sidle	

-idden

-idden

bedridden	hidden
forbidden	ridden

-iddle

-iddle

fiddle	middle	twiddle
griddle	riddle	

-ide

-ide		-ied	-eyed
alongside	side	applied	blue-eyed
aside	slide	cried	brown-eyed
beside	snide	denied	cross-eyed
bride	stride	died	green-eyed
collide	suicide	dissatisfied	
confide	tide	dried	-I'd
countryside	wide	fried	I'd
decide	worldwide	horrified	
divide		identified	-ighed
glide		implied	sighed
guide		justified	
hide		lied	
inside		occupied	
nationwide		qualified	
offside		replied	
outside		satisfied	
pride		terrified	
provide		tied	
ride		tried	
seaside		untied	

-ided

-ided
confided
decided
divided
guided
lopsided
misguided
one-sided
provided
undecided

Yes no, am I misguided?
No yes, I'm undecided.

-ider

-ider

cider	insider	provider	wider
glider	joyrider	rider	
hang-glider	outsider	spider	

-iding

-iding

colliding	dividing	hang-gliding	riding
confiding	gliding	hiding	sliding
deciding	guiding	providing	striding

-ie

Like the sound in the word die – look up -y^2 for words ending in this sound

-ied

Like the sound in the word cried – look up -ide for words ending in this sound

-ief

-ief	-eef	-eaf	-if
belief	beef	leaf	motif
brief	coral reef	overleaf	
chief	corned beef	sheaf	-ife
debrief	reef		Tenerife
disbelief	roast beef		
grief			
handkerchief			
relief			
thief			

-ield

Look up -ealed for words ending in this sound

-ies

Like the sound in the word cries – look up -ize for words ending in
this sound

-ieve

-ieve	-eive	-eave	-eeve
achieve	conceive	heave	sleeve
believe	deceive	leave	
disbelieve	perceive	weave	-e've
grieve	receive		we've
make-believe		-eve	
relieve		Eve	-ive
reprieve		Steve	naive
retrieve			
thieve			

-iever

-iever	-eaver	-ever	-eiver
achiever	beaver	fever	deceiver
believer	leaver	hayfever	receiver
disbeliever	school-leaver	lever	
retriever	weaver	scarlet fever	

-ife

-ife			
knife	paperknife	pocketknife	wife
life	penknife	rife	

-iff

-iff			-if
bored stiff	scared stiff	whiff	if
Cardiff	sniff		
cliff	stiff		

-ift

-ift			
drift	lift	shift	swift
gift	rift	sift	uplift

-ig

-ig			
big	gig	rig	twig
dig	jig	sprig	wig
fig	pig	swig	

-igger

-igger

bigger	snigger
digger	trigger
gravedigger	

-igour

rigour
vigour

-igure

figure

-iggle

-iggle

giggle	wiggle
jiggle	wriggle
niggle	
squiggle	

-ight

-ight

alight	right
all right	sight
Bonfire Night	slight
bright	starlight
candlelight	tight
delight	tonight
fight	uptight
flight	
fright	
Guy Fawkes Night	
knight	
light	
might	
moonlight	
night	
outright	
overnight	

-ite

appetite
bite
black-and-
  white
dynamite
excite
invite
kite
off-white
polite
quite
recite
rewrite
satellite
site
Snow White
spite
unite

white
write

-eight

height

-eit

Fahrenheit

-ighted

Look up -ited for words ending in this sound

-ighter

-ighter	-iter
brighter	screenwriter
bullfighter	scriptwriter
fighter	songwriter
firefighter	typewriter
highlighter	whiter
lighter	writer
tighter	

-ightly

-ightly	-itely
brightly	politely
fortnightly	
lightly	
nightly	
rightly	
slightly	
sprightly	
tightly	
unsightly	

-ike

-ike

alike
bike
businesslike
dislike
hike
like
lookalike
Mike
mike
motorbike
mountain bike
soundalike
spike

sportsmanlike
strike
take a hike
unlike

-yke

dyke

Some say that it's not **businesslike**
To go to work riding on a **bike**.

-iking

-iking

biking
disliking

hiking
liking

striking
Viking

-ile

-ile

compile
crocodile
fertile
file
hostile
juvenile
mile
missile
mobile

pile
profile
smile
sterile
stile
tile
versatile
vile
while

worthwhile

-aisle

aisle

-I'll

I'll

-isle

isle

-yle

style

-iling

-iling		-yling
compiling	tiling	styling
filing		
smiling		

-ility

-ility
ability
disability
possibility
responsibility

-ill

-ill		-il
Bill	refill	Brazil
bill	shrill	daffodil
brill	sill	nil
chill	skill	until
downhill	spill	
drill	still	
fill	thrill	
frill	till	
go downhill	uphill	
grill	Will	
hill	will	
if looks could kill	windowsill	
ill		
Jill		
kill		
mill		
pill		

-illa

-illa	-iller	-illar
Camilla	chiller	caterpillar
chinchilla	killer	pillar
flotilla	miller	
gorilla	painkiller	
guerrilla	thriller	
vanilla	weedkiller	
villa		

-illed

-illed		-ild
chargrilled	skilled	build
chilled	spilled	guild
drilled	strong-willed	women's guild
filled	thrilled	
grilled	weak-willed	
killed		

-iller

Look up -illa for words ending in this sound

-illing

-illing	
chilling	thrilling
drilling	unwilling
filling	willing
grilling	
killing	
spilling	

-illy

-illy	-ily	-illi
Billy	lily	chilli
chilly	water lily	
filly		
frilly		
hilly		
milly		
silly		

-ilt

-ilt		
built	quilt	tilt
guilt	spilt	well-built
kilt	stilt	

-ily

-ily	-yly	-ighly	-ylie
drily	shyly	highly	Kylie
wily	slyly		
		-iley	
		smiley	

-im

-im			-ym
brim	Muslim	Tim	gym
dim	prim	trim	
grim	rim		-ymn
him	skim	-imb	hymn
Jim	slim	limb	
Kim	swim		

-ime

-ime		-yme	-I'm
all-time	part-time	rhyme	I'm
chime	pastime	thyme	
crime	prime		
full-time	slime	-imb	
grime	springtime	climb	
half time	summertime		
just in time	time		
lime	wintertime		
meantime			
mime			
overtime			
pantomime			

They say to play in **pantomime**
It helps if you turn up on **time**.

-immer

-immer	
dimmer	slimmer
glimmer	swimmer
shimmer	trimmer
simmer	

-imp

-imp	
chimp	limp
crimp	shrimp
imp	wimp

-in

-in		-ine	-inn
aspirin	sin	feminine	inn
begin	skin	genuine	
bin	spin	masculine	
chin	thin	medicine	
din	tin		
Dublin	twin		
fin	violin		
gin	vitamin		
grin	win		
in	within		
pin			

-ina

-ina	-eaner	-ena	-eener
Argentina	cleaner	arena	greener
ballerina	leaner	hyena	keener
Sabrina	meaner	Ribena®	
Tina			

-ince

-ince		-inse
convince	since	rinse
mince	wince	
prince		

-inch

-inch		
clinch	flinch	pinch
finch	inch	

-ind¹

-ind	-inned	-ined
downwind	grinned	disciplined
Rosalind	sinned	
whirlwind	thick-skinned	
wind (=a gust of air)	tinned	

-ind²

-ind		-ined	-igned
behind	unkind	combined	designed
bind	unwind	confined	resigned
blind	wind (= to twist)	declined	signed
colour-blind		defined	
find		dined	
grind		fined	
hind		inclined	
humankind		lined	
kind		reclined	
mankind		refined	
mastermind		underlined	
mind		whined	
remind			
rewind			
rind			

-inder

-inder	
baby-minder	grinder
binder	kinder
childminder	minder
finder	reminder

-ine[1]

-ine

borderline	mine	twine	
brine	nine	underline	
Caroline	off-line	valentine	
combine	on-line	vine	
confine	pine	whine	
decline	porcupine	wine	
define	recline		
dine	refine		
fine	shine		
incline	spine		
line	swine		

-ign

design
resign
sign

-ine[2]

Like the sound in the word machine – look up -een for words ending in this sound

-ined

Like the sound in the word combined – look up -ind[2] for words ending in this sound

-iner

-iner	-ina	-inor	-ynah
diner	China	minor	mynah
eyeliner	china		
finer			
liner	-igner		
miner	designer		

-ing

-ing

anything	sling	string	wing
bring	spring	swing	wring
cling	sting	thing	
everything			
fling			
king			
ring			
sing			

> *Some angels **sing** of joy and **spring**,*
> *Some angels **sing** of **everything**.*

-inge

-inge

cringe	singe	whinge
fringe	tinge	
hinge	twinge	

-inger

-inger

bell-ringer	linger	swinger
dead ringer	ringer	winger
finger	singer	

-ining

-ining		-igning
combining	shining	designing
dining	underlining	resigning
lining	whining	signing
mining		
pining		
reclining		
refining		

-ink

-ink

blink	ink	shrink	wink
brink	link	sink	
clink	pink	stink	
drink	rink	think	

-inner

-inner

beginner	sinner
dinner	spinner
grinner	thinner
inner	winner
prizewinner	

-int

-int

fingerprint	peppermint	squint
flint	print	tint
glint	skint	
hint	spearmint	
mint	sprint	

-ion

-ion	-aiian	-ian	-iron
dandelion	Hawaiian	Brian	iron
lion			
Zion			-yan
			Ryan

-ip

-ip

championship	grip	quip	snip
chip	hip	relationship	strip
clip	lip	rip	tip
dip	membership	ship	trip
drip	nip	sip	unzip
felt-tip	paperclip	skip	whip
flip	pip	slip	zip

-ipe

-ipe

			-ype
bagpipe	pipe	swipe	hype
drainpipe	ripe	unripe	type
gripe	stripe	wipe	

-ipped

-ipped

chipped	gripped	slipped	whipped
clipped	nipped	snipped	zipped
dipped	quipped	stripped	
dripped	ripped	tipped	-ipt
equipped	sipped	tripped	script
flipped	skipped	unzipped	

-ipper

-ipper

clipper	kipper	slipper
dipper	paint-stripper	
flipper	skipper	

-ird

-ird		-erd	-ord
bird	referred	herd	the last word
blackbird	undeterred	nerd	word
hummingbird			
ladybird	-eard	-irred	-urd
third	heard	stirred	absurd
	overheard	whirred	lemon curd
-erred			
deterred			-urred
preferred			blurred

-ire

-ire	-ier		-igher
admire	amplifier	hairdryer	higher
backfire	drier	flyer	
campfire	flier	spin-dryer	-ior
desire	hairdrier	tumble-dryer	prior
dire	high-flier		
entire	spin-drier	-ia	-oir
fire	tumble-drier	via	choir
hire			
inquire	-yer	-iar	-uyer
inspire	dryer (=a	liar	buyer
perspire	device that		
require	dries		-yre
retire	something)		tyre
sapphire			
spire			
tire			
umpire			
vampire			
wire			

> The economy **flier** flew **higher** and **higher**
> Because she had money to spare,
> But as the plane landed I saw her **perspire**
> She's much happier in the air.

-ired

admired	hired	retired
backfired	inquired	tired
desired	inspired	wired
dog-tired	perspired	
fired	required	

-iring

admiring	inquiring	tiring
awe-inspiring	inspiring	uninspiring
desiring	perspiring	untiring
firing	requiring	
hiring	retiring	

-irl

-irl	-earl	-url
girl	earl	curl
swirl	mother-of-pearl	hurl
twirl	pearl	unfurl
whirl		

-irm

-irm	-erm	-orm
confirm	germ	ringworm
firm	perm	tapeworm
squirm	term	worm

-irst

-irst	-ursed	-orst	-urst
first	cursed	worst	burst
headfirst	nursed		
thirst			
	-earsed		
-ersed	rehearsed		
immersed			
reversed			

-irt

-irt	-ert		-urt
dirt	advert	insert	blurt
flirt	convert	pert	curt
miniskirt	desert (= to		hurt
shirt	leave)		spurt
skirt	dessert (= a		unhurt
squirt	sweet course)		
sweatshirt	divert		
T-shirt	exert		
underskirt			

-ise

Look up -ize for words ending in this sound

-ised

Look up -ized for words ending in this sound

-iser

Look up -izer for words ending in this sound

-ish

dish	goldfish	Scottish	wish
English	Irish	starfish	
fish	Jellyfish	swish	

-ising

Look up -izing for words ending in this sound

-ision

-ision

collision	revision	vision
decision	supervision	
division	television	

-isk

-isk

		-isc
brisk	hard disk	compact disc
disk	risk	disc
(= computer disk)	whisk	gold disc
floppy disk		platinum disc
frisk		silver disc

-ism

-ism

favouritism	pessimism
hypnotism	racism
journalism	terrorism
mechanism	vandalism
optimism	

-iss

-iss		-ice	-is
amiss	kiss	justice	Chris
bliss	miss	liquorice	this
dismiss	near miss	prejudice	
diss	Swiss		
hiss			

-ist

-st			-iced
assist	optimist	twist	prejudiced
consist	organist	wrist	
exist	persist		
feminist	pessimist	-issed	
fist	pianist	dismissed	
hypnotist	realist	hissed	
insist	receptionist	kissed	
journalist	resist	missed	
list	round the		
mist	twist		
motorist	scientist		
novelist	terrorist		

*I wrote a poem with a **twist**
And turned into a **novelist**.*

-ister

-ister		-istor
blister	sister	transistor
half-sister	stepsister	
Mister	twister	

-istic

-istic

artistic	realistic
optimistic	statistic
pessimistic	unrealistic

-it

-it

admit	lit
armpit	nit
baby-sit	omit
bedsit	permit
benefit	pit
bit	quit
blue tit	resit
Brit	sit
commit	slit
fit	spit
flit	split
grit	transmit
hit	unfit
it	Whit
keep-fit	wit
kit	
knit	

-ite

exquisite
hypocrite
infinite
opposite

-itt

Brad Pitt
mitt

To **benefit** from keeping **fit**
You'll need quite a **bit** of **grit**.

-itch

-itch

bewitch	stitch
ditch	switch
hitch	twitch
itch	witch
pitch	

-ich

enrich
rich
sandwich
which

-ite

Look up -ight for words ending in this sound

-ited

-ited
excited
invited
overexcited

recited
uninvited
united

-ighted
delighted
far-sighted
long-sighted

partially
sighted
short-sighted

-iter

Like the sound in the word writer – look up -ighter for words ending in this sound

-ith

-ith
goldsmith
pith

silversmith
Will Smith

with

-yth
myth

-ither

-ither
dither

slither

wither

-iting

-iting
backbiting
biting
exciting
handwriting
inviting
nail-biting

reciting
unexciting
uninviting
whiting
writing

-ighting
bullfighting
delighting
fighting
lighting
sighting

-ition

-ition	-ician	-ission	-icion
addition	beautician	admission	suspicion
ambition	electrician	mission	
competition	magician	omission	
composition	musician	permission	
condition	optician	transmission	
exhibition	politician		
expedition			
partition			
petition			
position			
superstition			
tradition			

A musician on a mission
Wrote a composition
In the classical tradition,
And he won a competition.

-itted

-itted		-ited
admitted	permitted	benefited
committed	quick-witted	
fitted	transmitted	
gritted		
knitted		
omitted		

-itter

-itter			-eter
baby-sitter	glitter	titter	barometer
bitter	gritter	transmitter	mileometer
fitter	litter	twitter	speedometer
fritter	quitter		thermometer

-itting

admitting
baby-sitting
close-fitting
committing
fitting
flitting
hitting

knitting
loose-fitting
omitting
permitting
quitting
side-splitting
sitting

slitting
spitting
splitting
tight-fitting
transmitting

-iting
benefiting

-ittle

-ittle
brittle
little

skittle
whittle

-it'll
it'll

-itty

-itty
bitty
ditty
gritty
kitty
witty

-ity
city
pity
self-pity

-etty
pretty

-ittee
committee

-ive¹

-ive
adjective
alternative
forgive
give
live (= to exist)

positive
relative
secretive
talkative

-ieve
sieve

*I cannot be **secretive**
Because I'm so **talkative**.*

-ive²

-ive

			-I've
alive	five	skive	I've
arrive	hive	survive	
contrive	jive	thrive	
deprive	live (= alive)		
dive	revive		
drive			

Don't cheat on the street
*if you want to **survive***
Just move to the beat
*and you will stay **alive**.*

-iver¹

-iver

deliver	quiver
giver	river
liver	shiver

-iver²

-iver

			-ivor
deep-sea diver	driver	skiver	survivor
diver	fiver	skydiver	

-iving¹

-iving

forgiving	living	thanksgiving
giving	prizegiving	

-iving²

-iving

arriving	driving	skydiving
depriving	reviving	surviving
diving	skiving	thriving

-ize

-ize	-ise	-ies	-ighs
apologize	advertise	cries	sighs
authorize	advise	denies	thighs
baptize	anti-clockwise	dies	
booby-prize	arise	dries	-uys
capsize	clockwise	flies	buys
economize	compromise	fries	guys
emphasize	despise	lies	
equalize	devise	qualifies	-yse
finalize	disguise	relies	analyse
hypnotize	exercise	replies	paralyse
idolize	guise	spies	
king-size	otherwise	tries	-yes
medium-size	prise (=to prise		dyes
memorize	something		
organize	open)		
prize (=a prize	revise		
in a competition	rise		
or = to value	supervise		
something)	surprise		
realize	televise		
recognize	unwise		
size	wise		
specialize			
sympathize			

-ized

-ized		-ised	-ysed
apologized	medium-sized	advertised	analysed
authorized	memorized	advised	paralysed
baptized	organized	compromised	
capsized	prized	despised	
civilized	realized	disguised	
emphasized	recognized	exercised	
equalized	specialized	revised	
fair-sized	sympathized	supervised	
finalized	unauthorized	surprised	
hypnotized	uncivilized	televised	
idolized			
king-sized			

-izer

-izer		-iser	-isor
equalizer	stabilizer	advertiser	supervisor
fertilizer		adviser	
liquidizer		miser	
moisturizer		wiser	
organizer			

-izing

-izing		-ising	
agonizing	hypnotizing	advising	surprising
apologizing	memorizing	advertising	
appetizing	organizing	arising	
capsizing	realizing	disguising	
emphasizing	recognizing	exercising	
equalizing	sympathizing	revising	
finalizing		rising	

-izz

-izz	-is	-iz	-s
fizz	his	quiz	Ms
swizz	is	showbiz	
whizz			

-o¹

-o	-ow	-oe	-oh
ago	below	doe	doh
banjo	blow	foe	oh
bravo	bow (= knot or	Joe	
buffalo	= weapon)	mistletoe	-ew
cameo	bungalow	toe	sew
cheerio	crow	woe	
domino	flow		-owe
Eskimo	Glasgow	-ough	owe
get-up-and-go	glow	although	
go	grow	dough	
hello	know	though	
no	low		
PTO	mow		
radio	Punch and		
Romeo	Judy show		
Scorpio	row (= a line of		
so	things or = to		
so-and-so	row a boat)		
studio	show		
to and fro	slow		
UFO	snow		
undergo	sow (= to sow		
video	seeds)		
	stow		
	throw		
	tow		
	window		

Go with the **flow** Joe
You **slow so-and-so**,
You're on **video**
Go on enjoy the **show**.

-o²

Like the sound in the word do – look up -ew for words ending in this sound

-oach

-oach
approach
coach
cockroach
poach
stagecoach

-ooch
brooch

-oad

Look up -owed[1] for words ending in this sound

-oaded

-oaded
downloaded
goaded
loaded
offloaded
unloaded

-oded
coded
exploded

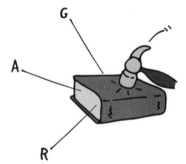

I hit the grammar with a hammer
My mind and pen were **loaded**,
The sentences began to stammer
And all the words **exploded**.

-oading

-oading
downloading
goading
loading

offloading
unloading

-oding
coding
exploding

-oal

Look up **-ole** for words ending in this sound

-oard

-oard
aboard
across-the-
board
blackboard
dartboard
dashboard
draughtboard
hoard
noticeboard
overboard
plasterboard
skateboard
skirting board
snowboard

-ord
afford
chord (=in
music)
cord (=string)

ford
landlord
lord
record
sword
tape-record
video-record
vocal cord

-ored
adored
bored
explored
ignored
restored
scored
snored
stored
unexplored

-awed
clawed
flawed
gnawed
overawed
pawed
sawed
thawed

-ard
award
reward
toward
ward

-aud
applaud
defraud
fraud

-oared
roared
soared

-oad
broad

-oored
floored

-orde
horde

-oured
poured

-oarding

-oarding	-arding	-auding	-ording
boarding	rewarding	applauding	recording
hoarding	unrewarding	marauding	tape-recording
skateboarding			
snowboarding			

-oast

Look up -ost² for words ending in this sound

-oaster

-oaster	-oster
boaster	poster
coaster	
toaster	

-oat

-oat		-ote
afloat	nanny-goat	banknote
billy-goat	overcoat	devote
boat	petticoat	dote
coat	raincoat	note
float	rowing boat	promote
gloat	scapegoat	quote
goat	speedboat	remote
jump down someone's throat	stoat	vote
	throat	wrote
	undercoat	
moat		
motorboat		

-oating

-oating	-oting
boating	doting
coating	noting
floating	quoting
gloating	voting

-ob

-ob			-ab
blob	knob	snob	swab
Bob	lob	sob	
corn on the cob	mob	throb	
heart-throb	nose job		
hob	Rob		
job	rob		
	slob		

-obble

-obble	-abble
bobble	squabble
cobble	
gobble	
hobble	
nobble	
wobble	

-obby

-obby	-obbie
blobby	Robbie
hobby	
knobby	
lobby	

-obe

-obe
bathrobe
globe
lobe
probe
robe

-ock

-ock			-och
block	frock	shuttlecock	loch
chip off the	knock	smock	
old block	lock	sock	-ok
chock-a-block	mock	stock	wok
clock	o'clock	unblock	
cock	padlock	unlock	
dock	rock		
crock	shamrock		
flock	shock		

-ocks

-ocks		-ox	
blocks	rocks	box	pox
clocks	shamrocks	brainbox	smallpox
cocks	shocks	chatterbox	
docks	shuttlecocks	chickenpox	-ochs
flocks	smocks	fox	lochs
frocks	socks	jack-in-the-box	
knocks	stocks	letterbox	-oks
locks	unblocks	matchbox	woks
mocks	unlocks	moneybox	
padlocks		ox	

-od

-od	-ad	-odd
clod	quad	odd
cod	squad	
God	wad	
god		
nod		
plod		
pod		
prod		
Rod		
rod		
sod		
trod		

-ode

Look up -owed[1] for words ending in this sound

-ody

-ody	-oddy
anybody	Noddy
body	shoddy
busybody	
everybody	
nobody	
somebody	

-oes

Look up -ose[2] for words ending in this sound

-off

-off	-ough
off	cough
scoff	whooping
well-off	cough

-og

-og		-ogue
bog	hog	catalogue
clog	jog	dialogue
cog	lapdog	
dog	log	
flog	slog	
fog	smog	
frog	underdog	

*If you want to buy a **dog***
*Don't get one from a **catalogue**,*
You may get ripped off in the end
It's best to buy one from a friend.

-oid

Look up -oyed for words ending in this sound

-oil

-oil			-oyle
boil	oil	spoil	gargoyle
castor oil	olive oil	toil	
coil	recoil		
foil	soil		

-oin

-oin
coin
join
loin
sirloin

-oint

-oint

appoint	joint
boiling point	point
cashpoint	power point
disappoint	sore point
freezing point	

-oke

-oke	-oak	-olk
awoke	cloak	folk
backstroke	croak	yolk
bloke	oak	
breaststroke	soak	
broke		
choke		
Coke®		
joke		
poke		
provoke		
smoke		
spoke		
stroke		
woke		
yoke		

-oken

awoken	soft-spoken	woken
broken	spoken	
heartbroken	token	
outspoken	well-spoken	

-oker

-oker	-oca	-ochre	-ocre
broker	tapioca	ochre	mediocre
choker			
joker			
non-smoker			
pawnbroker			
poker			
smoker			
stockbroker			

-oking

-oking		-oaking
broking	smoking	croaking
choking	stroking	soaking
joking	thought-	
non-smoking	provoking	
poking		
provoking		

-ol

-ol	-oll
aerosol	doll
alcohol	
parasol	

-old

-old	-olled	-oled	-owled
behold	controlled	consoled	bowled
bold	enrolled		
cold	patrolled	-ould	
fold	remote-	mould	
gold	controlled		
hold	rolled		
ice-cold	scrolled		
marigold	strolled		
old			
scold			
sold			
stone-cold			
told			
unfold			
withhold			

Buffaloes who compose prose
are something to behold
Like Eskimos who play banjos
they're worth their weight in gold.

-older

-older	-oulder
beholder	boulder
bolder	cold-shoulder
colder	shoulder
folder	smoulder
holder	
householder	
older	
record-holder	

-ole

-ole	-oal	-ol	-oul
armhole	charcoal	control	soul
bargepole	coal	enrol	
buttonhole	foal	patrol	-owl
casserole	goal	remote control	bowl
console	own goal	self-control	
cubbyhole	shoal		
flagpole			
hole	-oll		
manhole	poll		
mole	roll		
Nicole	scroll		
pigeonhole	stroll		
Pole	toll		
pole	troll		
pothole			
rigmarole			
role			
sole			
stole			
tadpole			
totem pole			
vole			
whole			

-olic

-olic

alcoholic	shopaholic
chocoholic	symbolic
colic	workaholic
frolic	
nonalcoholic	

-oll

Like the sound in the word roll – look up -ole for words ending in this sound

-ollar

-ollar	-olar
collar	scholar
dollar	

-oller

-oller	-ola	-olar	-oler
controller	cola	polar	potholer
roller	tombola	solar	
steamroller			-owler
stroller			bowler
molar			

-olling

-olling	-oling	-owling
controlling	consoling	bowling
enrolling	potholing	tenpin bowling
patrolling		
rolling		
scrolling		
strolling		

-olly

-olly	-olley	-ollie
brolly	trolley	collie
dolly		
folly		
golly		
Holly		
holly		
jolly		
lolly		

-olour

-olour	-uller
colour	duller
discolour	
off-colour	
watercolour	

-olt

-olt	-oult
bolt	moult
colt	
dolt	
jolt	
revolt	
thunderbolt	

-olve

-olve	
dissolve	resolve
evolve	revolve
involve	solve

-oly

-oly	-oalie	-oley	-olly
holy	goalie	holey	wholly
roly-poly			

	-olely	-oli	
-owly	solely	ravioli	
lowly			
slowly			

-om

-om	-omb
CD-ROM	bomb
from	
pompom	
Tom	

-oma

-oma	-oamer	-omber	-omer
aroma	roamer	beachcomber	Homer
coma			
diploma			

-ome[1]

-ome		-oam	-omb
dome	home	foam	comb
gnome	Rome	roam	honeycomb

-ome[2]

Like the sound in the word some – look up -um for words ending in this sound

-oming

-oming	-umbing	-umming
becoming	mind-numbing	drumming
coming	numbing	humming
homecoming	plumbing	strumming
incoming		
overcoming		
up-and-coming		

> My mum said that I should try **humming**
> Because
> My **drumming**'s becoming mind-numbing.

-on¹

-on		-one	-an
carry-on	odds-on	gone	swan
con	on	scone	
hands-on	spot-on	shone	-ohn
icon	stick-on		John
marathon	upon		
moron			

-on²

Like the sound in the word son – look up -un for words ending in this sound

-ond

-ond		-onned	-onde
beyond	pond	conned	blonde
blond	respond	donned	
bond			
correspond		-and	
fond		wand	
James Bond			

-onder

-onder	-ander
ponder	squander
yonder	wander

-one¹

-one		-oan	-ewn
accident-prone	tone	groan	sewn
alone	trombone	loan	
backbone	zone	moan	-ogne
bone			cologne
chaperone	-own		
clone	blown		
collarbone	flown		
cone	grown		
cyclone	known		
drone	mown		
hailstone	outgrown		
home alone	overgrown		
lone	own		
microphone	shown		
mobile phone	sown (= sown		
payphone	seeds)		
phone	thrown		
postpone	unknown		
prone	well-known		
saxophone			
skin and bone			
stone			
telephone			
throne			

Frederick was loved and **well-known**
Until he bought a **saxophone**,
He played and made an awful **drone**
And now poor Frederick lives **alone**.

-one²

Like the sound in the word done – look up -un for words ending in this sound

-ong

-ong

along	long	song
belong	prolong	strong
gong	prong	throng
Hong Kong	sarong	wrong

-oning

-oning	-oaning	-owning
cloning	groaning	disowning
droning	moaning	owning
phoning		
postponing		
stoning		
telephoning		
toning		
zoning		

-ony

-ony	-oni	-oany	-oney
bony	canneloni	moany	phoney
crony	macaroni		
phony			
pony			
stony			
Tony			

-oo

Look up -ew for words ending in this sound

-ood

-ood			-ould
adulthood	livelihood	sisterhood	could
brotherhood	manhood	stood	should
childhood	misunderstood	understood	would
fatherhood	motherhood	withstood	
good	neighbourhood	womanhood	
hood	parenthood	wood	
likelihood	Robin Hood		

-oof

-oof

aloof	hoof	showerproof
bulletproof	proof	spoof
flameproof	roof	waterproof
foolproof	shockproof	

-ook

-ook

bankbook	nook	took
book	notebook	undercook
brook	overcook	undertook
cook	overlook	
crook	overtook	
exercise book	pocketbook	
fishing hook	rook	
hook	scrapbook	
look	shook	
mistook	storybook	

-ool

-ool		-ule	-oul
Blackpool	swimming	capsule	ghoul
boarding	pool	molecule	
school	tool	mule	-oule
cool	uncool	overrule	cagoule
drool		ridicule	
fool		rule	-ou'll
high school			you'll
ice-cool			
Liverpool			
paddling pool			
pool			
primary school			
school			
spool			
stool			

-oom

-oom	-ume	-omb	-om
bathroom	assume	tomb	whom
bloom	consume	womb	
boom	fume		
broom	perfume		
changing	presume		
room	resume		
classroom			
darkroom			
doom			
gloom			
groom			
loom			
room			
zoom			

Words can be powerful
And very meaningful
Therefore **assume**
They can also bring **gloom**.

-oon

-oon			-une
afternoon	festoon	saloon	dune
baboon	harpoon	soon	immune
balloon	honeymoon	soupspoon	June
bassoon	hot-air balloon	spoon	prune
boon	maroon	swoon	tune
buffoon	monsoon	tablespoon	
cartoon	moon	teaspoon	
cocoon	noon	tycoon	
croon	platoon	typhoon	
dessertspoon	raccoon		

-ooned

-ooned	-ound	-uned
ballooned	wound (= an injury)	tuned
cocooned		
festooned		
marooned		
swooned		

-oop

-oop		-oup
coop	snoop	group
droop	stoop	playgroup
hoop	swoop	soup
loop	troop	
scoop	whoop	

-oor[1]

Like the sound in the word poor – look up -ure for words ending in this sound

-oor²

Like the sound in the word door – look up -ore for words ending
in this sound

-oose

Like the sound in the word loose – look up -uce for words ending
in this sound

-oot¹

-oot	-ut
afoot	Lilliput
barefoot	put
foot	
soot	
underfoot	

-oot²

Like the sound in the word boot – look up -ute for words ending in
this sound

-ooter

-ooter	-uter	-euter	-uitor
hooter	computer	neuter	suitor
looter	cuter		
peashooter		-ewter	-utor
scooter		pewter	tutor
sharpshooter			
shooter			
troubleshooter			

-ooth

Look up -uth for words ending in this sound

-op

-op			-ap
belly-flop	hip-hop	pop	swap
blow your top	hop	prop	
bus stop	laptop	raindrop	
chop	lollipop	shop	
cop	mop	stop	
crop	non-stop	top	
drop	over-the-top		
flop	plop		

-ope

-ope	-oap
antelope	soap
cope	
dope	
elope	
envelope	
grope	
hope	
horoscope	
microscope	
mope	
pope	
rope	
scope	
slope	
telescope	

When I'm not sure if I can **cope**
I sit and read my **horoscope**.

-opper

-opper

chopper
come a
  cropper
copper
grasshopper
knee-high to a
  grasshopper
name-dropper
popper
shopper
spacehopper
stopper

whopper
window-
  shopper

-oper

improper
proper

-opping

-opping

chopping
cropping
dropping
flopping
hopping
name-
  dropping
popping
shopping
stopping

topping
whopping
window-
  shopping

-apping

swapping

-oppy

-oppy
choppy
floppy
poppy

sloppy
soppy
stroppy

-opy
copy
photocopy

-oral

-oral
coral
immoral
moral
oral

-arrel
quarrel

-aurel
laurel

-ord

Like the sound in the word lord – look up -oard for words ending in this sound

-order

-order
border
camcorder
disorder
order
recorder
reorder
tape recorder
video recorder

-oarder
boarder
hoarder
keyboarder

-arder
warder

-oader
broader

-ore

-ore	-aw	-or	-ar
adore	brother-in-law	ambassador	tug-of-war
before	caw	corridor	war
bore	claw	for	
core	daughter-in-law	labrador	**-awe**
evermore		nor	awe
explore	draw	or	overawe
fore	father-in-law		
furthermore	flaw	**-oor**	**-aur**
galore	gnaw	door	dinosaur
ignore	jackdaw	door-to-door	
more	jaw	floor	**-awer**
pinafore	law	next-door	drawer
restore	mother-in-law	trapdoor	
score	paw		**-orps**
shore	raw	**-oar**	**corps** (= a unit
Singapore	saw	boar	in the army)
snore	sister-in-law	oar	
sore	son-in-law	roar	**-ou're**
store	straw	soar	you're
superstore	thaw		
swore	the final straw	**-our**	
tore	withdraw	four	
wore		pour	
		your	

> He **swore** that he **saw** me dancing **before**
> Around **Singapore** with his **son-in-law**.

132

-ored

Look up -oard for words ending in this sound

-ores

Look up -aws for words ending in this sound

-oring

-oring	-oaring	-arring	-ouring
adoring	roaring	warring	pouring
boring	soaring		
exploring		-ooring	
ignoring		flooring	
poring			
restoring			
scoring			
snoring			
storing			

-ork[1]

-ork		-irk	-erk
artwork	waxwork	irk	berserk
bodywork	woodwork	quirk	jerk
fieldwork	work	shirk	perk
framework		smirk	
handiwork			-urk
metalwork			lurk
needlework			
overwork			
paperwork			
patchwork			

-ork²

Like the sound in the word cork – look up -alk for words ending in this sound

-orm

-orm		-arm
deform	thunderstorm	swarm
form	transform	warm
inform	uniform	
perform		
reform		
snowstorm		
storm		

-ormed

-ormed		-armed
deformed	reformed	swarmed
formed	stormed	warmed
informed	transformed	
performed		

-ormer

-ormer	-armer	-auma
former	warmer	trauma
informer		
performer		
reformer		

-orming

-orming	-arming
forming	global
performing	warming
storming	swarming
transforming	warming

-orn

-orn	-awn	-aun	-arn
acorn	brawn	faun (=a	warn
adorn	Dawn	fairytale	
born	dawn	creature)	-ean
corn	drawn	leprechaun	Sean
forlorn	fawn (=a	Shaun	
horn	young deer or		-ourn
reborn	= light brown)		mourn
scorn	lawn		
sweetcorn	pawn		
sworn	prawn		
thorn	sawn		
torn	spawn		
unicorn	withdrawn		
worn	yawn		

-orny

-orny	-awny
corny	brawny
horny	scrawny
thorny	tawny

-orse

-orse	-orce	-auce	-oarse
carthorse	divorce	sauce	coarse
gorse	enforce	soy sauce	hoarse
hobbyhorse	force	tomato sauce	
horse	reinforce		
Morse		**-ourse**	
remorse		course	
rocking horse		resource	
		source	

-ort

-ort		-ought	-aught
consort	snort	bought	caught
contort	sort	brought	taught
distort	spoilsport	fought	
escort	sport	nought	**-art**
export	support	ought	thwart
fort	transport	sought	wart
import		thought	
life-support			**-ourt**
passport		**-aut**	court
port		astronaut	
report		cosmonaut	
resort		taut	
retort			
short			

-ortion

-ortion		-aution
contortion	proportion	caution
distortion		precaution
portion		

-ory

-ory	-orey
glory	multistorey
gory	storey
Rory	
story	
Tory	

> The concrete **multi-storey**
> Shone in all its **glory**.

-ose¹

-ose	-oss
close (= near)	gross
dose	
morose	

-ose²

-ose		-oes	-ows
arose	suppose	buffaloes	blows
chose	those	dominoes	bows (= knots
close (= to		goes	or = weapons)
shut)		toes	rows (= lines
compose		tread on	or = rows a
enclose		someone's	boat)
expose		toes	shows
get up			sows (= sows
someone's			seeds)
nose		-os	
hose		banjos	
nose		cameos	-oze
oppose		Eskimos	doze
pose		radios	froze
propose		studios	
prose			
rose			

-osed

-osed
closed
composed
exposed
opposed
posed

proposed
supposed

-ozed
dozed

-osh

-osh
gosh
Josh
posh

slosh

-ash
brainwash
carwash
squash

wash

-osing

-osing
closing
composing
enclosing
exposing
hosing

opposing
posing
proposing

-ozing
dozing

-oss

-oss
across
albatross
boss
candyfloss
cross
double-cross
gloss

loss
moss
Ross
toss

-os
DOS

-ost[1]

-ost	-ossed
cost	crossed
defrost	tossed
frost	
long-lost	
lost	
low-cost	

-ost[2]

-ost	-oast	-ossed
furthermost	boast	engrossed
ghost	coast	
host	roast	
innermost	toast	
most		
post		
topmost		
uppermost		
utmost		

-osy

-osy	-osey	-osie	-ozy
cosy	nosey	Rosie	dozy
nosy			
posy			
rosy			

-ot

-ota

-otch

-ote

Look up -oat for words ending in this sound

-oth

-oth

| broth | dishcloth | moth |
| cloth | froth | tablecloth |

-other

-other

another	great-	smother
Big Brother	grandmother	stepbrother
brother	half-brother	stepmother
godmother	mother	
grandmother	other	

-otion

-otion

commotion	motion	-ocean
devotion	notion	ocean
emotion	potion	
lotion	promotion	

-otter

-otter

blotter	plotter	-atter
globetrotter	potter	squatter
Harry Potter	rotter	
hotter	totter	
jotter	trainspotter	
otter	trotter	

-otty

-otty

| dotty | knotty | spotty |
| grotty | potty | |

-ouch

-ouch

| couch | grouch | pouch |
| crouch | ouch | slouch |

-oud

Like the sound in the word proud – look up -owed^2 for words ending in this sound

-ough^1

Like the sound in the word rough – look up -uff for words ending in this sound

-ough^2

Like the sound in the word plough – look up -ow^2 for words ending in this sound

-ought

Look up -ort for sounds ending in this sound

-ounce

-ounce

announce
bounce
flounce
ounce
pounce
pronounce

-ound

-ound

all-round
around
astound
background
battleground
bound
compound
deerhound
found
foxhound
greyhound
ground
hound
merry-go-round

mound
playground
pound
profound
round
runaround
sound
surround
underground
unsound
unwound
wolfhound
wound (= past tense of wind)

-owned

browned
drowned
frowned
renowned

-ounding

-ounding

astounding
bounding
grounding
hounding

pounding
rounding
sounding
surrounding

143

-ount

-ount

account	count	mount
amount	discount	

-our

Like in the sound in the word sour – look up -ower[2] for words ending in this sound

-ous

-ous	-us	-as	-os
dangerous	abacus	good King	rhinoceros
fabulous	asparagus	Wenceslas	
famous	bus	Nicholas	
glamorous	discus		
gluttonous	genius	-uss	
hazardous	hippopotamus	discuss	
ludicrous	minibus	fuss	
marvellous	octopus		
mischievous	plus		
miraculous	terminus		
poisonous	thus		
scandalous	us		
timorous			

We must **discuss** the **genius**
Of Hip the **hippopotamus**.
He's **fabulous** and **marvellous**.
He's **glamorous** and so **famous**.

-ouse¹

-ouse

dormouse
farmhouse
fieldmouse
greenhouse
grouse
hothouse
house (= a
home)
house-to-
house

louse
madhouse
Mickey Mouse
mouse
playhouse
spouse
summerhouse
town house

-ouse²

Like the sound in the word blouse – look up -ows² for words
ending in this sound

-out

-out

about
all-out
bout
Brussels sprout
burnt-out
clout
devout
down-and-out
handout
hang-out
layabout
layout
lout
out

out-and-out
pout
roundabout
scout
shout
snout
spout
sprout
stout
thought-out
throughout
trout
walkabout
way-out

well-thought-
out
without

-oubt

doubt

-ought

drought

-outh[1]

-outh
mouth
south

-outh[2]

Like the sound in the word youth – look up -uth for words ending in this sound

-ove[1]

-ove			-auve
clove	grove	wove	mauve
cove	stove		
drove	treasure-trove		

-ove[2]

-ove		
above	glove	shove
dove	love	

-ove[3]

-ove	-oove	-ou've
approve	groove	you've
disapprove		
improve		
move		
prove		
remove		

-over¹

clover	leftover	pullover	stopover
Dover	moreover	pushover	turnover
going-over	once-over	rollover	voice-over
hangover	over	rover	walkover

-over²

-over

cover	lover	uncover
discover	recover	undercover

-oving

-oving

approving	improving	proving
disapproving	moving	removing

-ow¹

Like the sound in the word flow – look up -o¹ for words ending in this sound

-ow²

-ow		-ough	-aow
allow	now	bough	miaow
anyhow	ow	plough	
bow (= to bend down)	row (= an argument)	snowplough	
brow	sow (= a female pig)		
cow			
disallow	vow		
how	wow		

-owed¹

-owed	-oad	-ode	-ewed
crowed	download	code	sewed
glowed	goad	episode	
mowed	load	explode	-oed
owed	offload	mode	pigeon-toed
rowed (=	road	ode	
rowed a boat)	toad	rode	
showed	unload	strode	
snowed			
sowed			
stowed			
towed			

-owed²

-owed	-oud	-aowed	-owd
allowed	aloud	miaowed	crowd
bowed	cloud		
cowed	loud	-oughed	
disallowed	proud	ploughed	
rowed (=	rain cloud		
argued)	thundercloud		
vowed			

> We all stood **proud**
> We sang **aloud**
> We were a large and soulful **crowd**.

-owel

-owel	
bowel	trowel
dishtowel	vowel
towel	

-ower¹

-ower	-oer	-oa
blower	churchgoer	boa
flamethrower	cinema-goer	
grower	moviegoer	
lawnmower	theatre-goer	
lower (= further down)		
mower		
rower		
slower		
thrower		

-ower²

-ower		-our	
brainpower	sunflower	cornflour	self-raising flour
cauliflower	superpower	devour	sour
cower	tower	flour	sweet-and-sour
flower	wallflower	hour	
glower	willpower	our	
overpower		plain flour	
power		scour	
shower			

-owing

-owing		-oing	-ewing
blowing	rowing (= propelling a boat)	easy-going	sewing
flowing		going	
glowing	showing	ongoing	
growing	sowing	outgoing	
knowing	throwing		
mowing			
owing			

-owl

-owl	-oul
fowl	foul
growl	
howl	
owl	
prowl	
scowl	
waterfowl	
yowl	

-own[1]

Like the sound in the word grown – look up -one[1] for words ending in this sound

-own[2]

-own			-oun
bogged down	drown	tumbledown	noun
breakdown	evening gown	upside down	
brown	frown		
Charlie Brown	gown		
clown	lie-down		
crown	put-down		
down	run-down		
dressing-gown	town		

-ows[1]

Like the sound in the word shows – look up -ose[2] for words ending in this sound

-ows[2]

-ows	-ouse	-oughs	-owse
allows	arouse	boughs	browse
bows (= bends down)	blouse	ploughs	drowse
brows	rouse	snowploughs	
cows			-aows
disallows			miaows
rows (= arguments)			
sows (= female pigs)			
vows			

-ox

Look up -ocks for words ending in this sound

-oy

-oy		-oi	-uoy
ahoy	pride and joy	oi	buoy
alloy	schoolboy		
annoy	soy		
blue-eyed boy	Tannoy®		
boy	toy		
choirboy			
coy			
decoy			
destroy			
employ			
enjoy			
joy			
pageboy			
ploy			

-oyed

-oyed	-oid
annoyed	avoid
destroyed	cuboid
employed	paranoid
enjoyed	Polaroid®
overjoyed	tabloid
self-employed	
unemployed	

-ub

-ub			
club	hub	scrub	stub
cub	pub	shrub	sub
grub	rub	snub	tub

-ubby

-ubby		
chubby	hubby	stubby
grubby	scrubby	tubby

-uce

-uce	-oose	-use	-uice
introduce	goose	abuse (= bad treatment)	juice
produce	loose		sluice
reduce	moose	excuse (= a reason)	
reproduce	noose		-ousse
spruce		misuse (= wrong use)	mousse
truce		use (= a use of something)	

-uck

-ucked

Look up -uct for words ending in this sound

-ucker

-uckle

-uckling

-ucky

happy-go-
 lucky
lucky
mucky
plucky
unlucky
yucky

-uct

-uct	-ucked
abduct	chucked
conduct	clucked
construct	ducked
deduct	plucked
duct	sucked
instruct	tucked
obstruct	
product	
self-destruct	

-uction

-uction	
abduction	reduction
construction	reproduction
deduction	suction
destruction	
instruction	
introduction	
obstruction	
production	
reconstruction	

-ud

-ud	-ood
bud	blood
dud	flood
mud	
spud	
stick-in-the mud	
stud	
thud	

-uddy

-uddy	-udy	-oody
buddy	study	bloody
fuddy-duddy	understudy	
muddy		
ruddy		

-ude

-ude	-ewed	-ood	-ewd
conclude	brewed	brood	shrewd
crude	renewed	food	
dude	reviewed	mood	-ou'd
exclude	stewed		you'd
include	viewed	-eud	
intrude		feud	-ued
multitude			subdued
nude			
prude			
rude			

A good Samaritan gave **food**
To the hungry **multitude**.

155

-udge

begrudge	judge
budge	nudge
drudge	sludge
fudge	smudge
grudge	trudge

-ue

Look up **-ew** for words ending in this sound

-uel

-uel	-ewal	-ewel	-ual
cruel	renewal	jewel	dual
duel			
fuel			

-uff

-uff		-ough
bluff	scruff	enough
buff	scuff	rough
cuff	snuff	tough
fluff	stuff	
gruff		
handcuff		
huff		
muff		
off-the-cuff		
puff		
ruff		

> The poet was very knock-kneed
> His fingers could not move at speed,
> His wordplay was **rough**
> Concentrating was **tough**
> So his rhymes could not be guaranteed.

-uffer

-uffer	-ougher
bluffer	rougher
buffer	tougher
duffer	
gruffer	
puffer	
suffer	

-uffle

-uffle		
duffle	reshuffle	snuffle
kerfuffle	ruffle	shuffle
muffle	scuffle	truffle

-uffy

-uffy	-oughie
Buffy	toughie
fluffy	
huffy	
puffy	
scruffy	
stuffy	

-ug

-ug			
bug	jug	rug	tug
chug	litterbug	shrug	unplug
dug	lug	slug	
drug	mug	smug	
hearthrug	plug	snug	
hug	pug	thug	

-uit

Like the sound in the word suit – look up -ute for words ending in this sound

-uke

-uke	-ook
duke	gobbledygook
fluke	spook
Luke	
rebuke	

-ul

-ul		-ull	-ool
armful	powerful	bull	dyed-in-the-wool
colourful	purposeful	full	
faithful	sorrowful	like a red rag to a bull	wool
fanciful	tactful		
handful	thankful	pull	
harmful	unfaithful		
helpful	wonderful		
meaningful			
pitiful			

-ule

Like the sound in the word rule – look up -ool for words ending in this sound

-ulge

bulge   overindulge
indulge

-ulk

-ulk
bulk
hulk
sulk
The Hulk

-ull¹

-ull
dull   lull
gull   seagull
Hull   skull
hull

-ull²

Like the sound in the word full – look up -ul for words ending in
this sound

-ult

-ult
adult
catapult
consult
cult
insult
result

-uly

-uly
duly
truly
unduly
unruly

-ewly
newly

I tell you **truly**
I'm not **unruly**
Or troublesome
Just ask my mum.

-um

-um
bubble gum
chewing gum
chrysan-
  themum
chum
drum
glum
gum
hum
kettledrum
maximum
medium
minimum
mum
pendulum
platinum
plum

rum
scrum
scum
slum
strum
sum
swum
tum
yum-yum

-ome
become
come
meddlesome
overcome
quarrelsome
some
tiresome
troublesome

-umb
crumb
dumb
numb
plumb
thumb
Tom Thumb

-umber

cucumber
lumber
number
outnumber
slumber

-umble

-umble

crumble	rumble
fumble	stumble
grumble	tumble
humble	
jumble	
mumble	
rough-and- tumble	

-umbling

-umbling

crumbling	mumbling
bumbling	rumbling
fumbling	stumbling
grumbling	tumbling
jumbling	

-ume

Look up -oom for words ending in this sound

-ummer

-ummer	-omer	-umber
drummer	latecomer	plumber
glummer	newcomer	
midsummer		
strummer		
summer		

-ummy

-ummy
chummy
dummy
mummy
plummy
tummy
yummy

-ump

-ump			
bump	grump	pump	trump
chump	hump	rump	
clump	jump	slump	
dump	lump	stump	
frump	plump	thump	

-umpy

-umpy	
bumpy	jumpy
dumpy	lumpy
frumpy	stumpy
grumpy	

-un

-un	-one	-on	-onne
aftersun	anyone	godson	tonne
begun	done	grandson	
bun	everyone	great-	
fun	none	grandson	
gun	one	son	
hit-and-run	outdone	stepson	
machine gun	overdone	ton	
nun	redone	won	
outrun	undone		
overrun			
pun			
run			
shotgun			
shun			
spun			
stun			
sun			

-unch

-unch	
bunch	munch
brunch	Punch
crunch	punch
hunch	scrunch
lunch	

-und

-und	-unned
fund	shunned
refund	stunned

-under

-under	-onder
blunder	wonder
down under	
plunder	
thunder	
under	

-une

Look up -oon for words ending in this sound

-ung

-ung		-ong	-ung
bung	strung	among	young
clung	stung		
dung	sung	-ongue	
flung	swung	tongue	
hung	wrung		
lung			
rung			
slung			
sprung			

*How great that song when it is **sung**,*
*It's like sweet nectar on my **tongue**.*

-unk

-unk		-onk
bunk	shrunk	monk
chunk	skunk	
drunk	slunk	
funk	stunk	
hunk	sunk	
junk	trunk	
punk		

-unky

-unky	-onkey
chunky	monkey
funky	
hunky	

A very **hunky funky monkey**
Ate a lot and then got **chunky**.

-unner

-unner
gunner
runner
stunner

-unning

-unning	
cunning	running
outrunning	shunning
overrunning	stunning

-unny

-unny	-oney	-onny
bunny	honey	sonny
funny	money	
runny		
sunny		
unfunny		

-unt

-unt	-ont
blunt	confront
brunt	front
grunt	upfront
headhunt	waterfront
hunt	
manhunt	
punt (= a boat)	
runt	
shunt	
stunt	

-up

-up		
built-up	made-up	summing-up
buttercup	mixed-up	sup
coffee cup	pick-me-up	teacup
cover-up	pup	up
cup	rolled-up	washing-up
follow-up	runner-up	
grown-up	stand-up	
jumped-up	stuck-up	

-upt

-upt	-upped
abrupt	cupped
bankrupt	supped
corrupt	upped
disrupt	
erupt	
interrupt	

-ur

-ur	-er	-ir	-irr
blur	deter	fir	whirr
fur	her	sir	
occur	prefer	stir	-urr
slur	refer		purr
spur	transfer	-ere	
		were	-yrrh
			myrrh

-ure

-ure		-oor	-our
allure	pure	boor	tour
assure	reassure	moor	
cure	secure	poor	
demure	signature		
endure	sure		
ensure	temperature		
furniture	unsure		
immature			
impure			
insecure			
insure			
literature			
lure			
manicure			
mature			
miniature			
obscure			
overture			
premature			

Be **sure** that great art will **endure**
Longer than plastic **furniture**.

167

-urely

-urely
demurely
insecurely
obscurely
prematurely
purely
securely
surely

-oorly
poorly

-uring

-uring
alluring
assuring
curing
during
enduring

ensuring
insuring
luring
reassuring

-ooring
mooring

-ouring
touring

-urn

-urn
about-turn
burn
churn
overturn
return
Saturn

spurn
turn
urn
U-turn

-earn
earn
learn
yearn

-ern
concern
fern
stern

-urried

-urried
curried
hurried
scurried

-orried
worried

-urry

-urry	-orry	-urrey
curry	worry	Surrey
flurry		
hurry		
scurry		

-urt

Look up -irt for words ending in this sound

-us

Look up -ous for words ending in this sound

-use

-use	-ews	-oos	-oose
abuse (= to treat badly)	crews	boos	choose
accuse	mews	zoos	
amuse	news		-o's
confuse		-ose	who's
excuse (= to forgive)	-ooze	lose (= to misplace or = to be beaten)	-ues
fuse	booze		blues
misuse (= to use wrongly)	ooze	whose	
muse	snooze		-wos
refuse (= to not accept or not allow)		-uise	twos
reuse (= to use again)		bruise	
ruse		cruise	
use (= to use)			

-user

-user
accuser
user

-uiser
bruiser
cruiser

-oser
loser

-ush¹

-ush
blush
brush
clothes brush
crush
flush
gush
hairbrush
hush
lush
nailbrush
paintbrush
plush
rush
scrubbing brush
slush
sweeping brush
thrush
toothbrush

-ush²

-ush
ambush
bush
George W Bush
push
shush

-using

-using
abusing
accusing
amusing
confusing
excusing
misusing
musing
refusing
reusing
using

-oozing
oozing
snoozing

-uising
bruising
cruising

-oosing
choosing

-osing
losing

-usk

-usk

busk	husk	rusk
dusk	musk	tusk

-ust

-ust			-ussed
adjust	gust	rust	concussed
bite the dust	just	thrust	discussed
bust	mistrust	trust	fussed
crust	must	unjust	
disgust	robust		
distrust			
dust			
entrust			

*If the world seems so **unjust***
*The people won't know who to **trust**.*

-uster

-uster

bluster	duster	muster
cluster	fluster	

-ustle

-ustle	-uscle	-ussel	-ussle
bustle	muscle	mussel	tussle
hustle			
rustle			

-usty

-usty

crusty	gusty	trusty
dusty	rusty	

-ut

-ut

			-utt
Brazil nut	gut	peanut	butt
but	halibut	rut	mutt
clean-cut	hazelnut	shut	putt
clear-cut	hut	strut	
coconut	jut	walnut	
cut	monkey nut		
do your nut	nut		

-utch

-utch		-uch	-ouch
clutch	Dutch	much	touch
crutch	hutch	such	

-ute

-ute		-oot	-ewt
absolute	pollute	boot	newt
acute	prosecute	hoot	
brute	salute	loot	-oute
chute	substitute	root	route
compute		scoot	
cute	-uit	shoot	
dilute	birthday suit	uproot	
dispute	fruit		
electrocute	grapefruit		
execute	pursuit		
flute	recruit		
institute	star fruit		
minute (= tiny)	suit		
mute	swimsuit		
parachute	tracksuit		
persecute			

-uth

-uth		-outh	-ooth
Ruth	untruth	uncouth	tooth
truth		youth	

-utter

-utter			
butter	gutter	putter	sputter
clutter	mutter	shutter	stutter
flutter	nutter	splutter	utter

-utton

-utton		
belly-button	glutton	push-button
button	mutton	unbutton

-uty

-uty	-ooty	-eauty	-uity
duty	booty	beauty	fruity
heavy-duty	snooty		
off-duty			

-uzz

-uzz	-oes
buzz	does
fuzz	

-uzzle

-uzzle			
guzzle	muzzle	nuzzle	puzzle

-y¹

-y

actually	Germany	quietly
agency	gradually	raspberry
agony	honestly	sanctuary
Amy	hopefully	secondary
apparently	Hungary	secondly
balcony	imaginary	secretly
carefully	immediately	strawberry
casually	injury	suddenly
category	Italy	sympathy
celebrity	January	totally
celery	jealousy	tragedy
century	jewellery	unfortunately
certainly	jokingly	urgently
comedy	lavatory	watery
company	library	willingly
cutlery	lovely	
deliberately	Lucy	
destiny	misery	
dictionary	nastily	
difficulty	naturally	
ecstasy	nervously	
elderly	obviously	
Emily	occasionally	
enemy	ordinary	
energy	penalty	
eventually	personally	
exactly	poetry	
February	poverty	
fidgety	primary	
finally	privacy	
fortunately	probably	
funnily	property	

-ee

agree
bee
chimpanzee
degree
disagree
fee
free
guarantee
knee
Lee
pee
referee
refugee
see
tee-hee
three
tree
Tweedledum and Tweedledee
wee

-e	-ie	-i	-ey
be	Charlie	broccoli	key
Chloe	Julie	ski	
he	Sophie		-G
me	Stephanie	-T	PG
PE		ICT	
RE	-D	IT	-P
recipe	CD		MP
she	DVD	-ay	
we	ID	quay	

-ea	-V	-C
pea	CV	BBC
plea	ITV	
sea	TV	
tea		

The wise man gave the **refugee**
A cup of tea and **sanctuary**.
And then upon the **balcony**
They read some profound **poetry**.
The wise man listened **carefully**
To tales of woe and **tragedy**.
The refugee, quite **naturally**
Was simply happy to be **free**.

-y²

-y		-ie	-igh
ally	spy	die	high
apply	stand-by	lie	sigh
awry	stir-fry	magpie	thigh
butterfly	supply	pie	
by	try	tie	-eye
cry	why	untie	eye
defy	wry		Popeye
deny		-ye	
dry		bye	-uy
fly		dye	buy
fry		goodbye	guy
horrify		rye	
identify		stye	
imply			
July		-i	
justify		hi	
multiply		I	
my		rabbi	
nearby			
notify			
occupy			
passer-by			
qualify			
rely			
reply			
satisfy			
shy			
simplify			
sky			
sly			

-ying

-ying	-ighing	-uying	-yeing
applying	sighing	buying	dyeing
crying			
defying			
denying			
drying			
dying			
flying			
frying			
horrifying			
identifying			
implying			
justifying			
lying			
multiplying			
notifying			
occupying			
qualifying			
relying			
replying			
satisfying			
simplifying			
spying			
supplying			
terrifying			
trying			
tying			
untying			

The poet just couldn't stop **crying**
Because there was just no **denying**,
This book his great friend
Had come to an end,
But he thought it was really worth **buying**.

Index

Here is an alphabetical list of the rhyming words in this dictionary, and the headings you will find them under.

at	-at	backfired	-ired	barmaid	-ade
ate	-ate	background	-ound	barn	-arn
athlete	-eat	backpack	-ack	barnyard	-ard
athletic	-etic	backpacks	-acks	barometer	-itter
atmosphere	-ear²	backs	-acks	barred	-ard
attach	-atch	backstage	-age	Barry	-arry
attack	-ack	backstroke	-oke	Bart	-art
attacked	-act	backwater	-ater¹	barter	-arter
attacks	-acks	backyard	-ard	base	-ace
attempt	-empt	bacon	-aken	based	-aced
attend	-end	bacteria	-erior	bash	-ash
attendant	-endant	bad	-ad	basketball	-all
attending	-ending	bag	-ag	bass (deep sound)	-ace
attention	-ention	Baghdad	-ad	bass (fish)	-ass¹
attic	-ick	bagpipe	-ipe	bassoon	-oon
attract	-act	bail	-ail	bat	-at
attraction	-action	bait	-ate	batch	-atch
aubergine	-een	bake	-ake	Bath	-ath
aunt	-ant	baker	-aker	bath	-ath
authorize	-ize	baking	-aking	bathrobe	-obe
authorized	-ized	balcony	-y¹	bathroom	-oom
autograph	-aph	ball	-all	Batman	-an
automatic	-ick	ballerina	-ina	batter	-atter
avenue	-ew	balloon	-oon	battlefield	-ealed
avoid	-oyed	ballooned	-ooned	battleground	-ound
awake	-ake	ballyhoo	-ew	batty	-atty
awaken	-aken	balm	-arm	bawl	-all
awaking	-aking	bamboo	-ew	bawling	-alling
award	-oard	ban	-an	bay	-ay
aware	-are	band	-and	bays	-ays
away	-ay	bandana	-anner	bazaar	-ar
awe	-ore	bandanna	-anner	BBC	-y¹
awe-inspiring	-iring	bang	-ang	be	-y¹
awoke	-oke	banger	-anger¹	beach	-each
awoken	-oken	bangle	-angle	beachcomber	-oma
awry	-y²	banjo	-o¹	bead	-eed
axe	-acks	banjos	-ose²	beading	-eeding
		bank	-ank	beady	-eedy
B		bankbook	-ook	beak	-eak
baa	-ar	banknote	-oat	beaker	-eaker
baboon	-oon	bankrupt	-upt	beam	-eam
baby-faced	-aced	banned	-and	bean	-een
baby-minder	-inder	banner	-anner	bear	-are
baby-sit	-it	baptize	-ize	bearer	-earer
baby-sitter	-itter	baptized	-ized	bearing	-aring
baby-sitting	-itting	bar	-ar	beast	-eased¹
back	-ack	barbecue	-ew	beat	-eat
backache	-ake	bard	-ard	beaten	-eaten
backbiting	-iting	bare	-are	beater	-eater
backbone	-one¹	barefoot	-oot¹	beating	-eating
backbreaking	-aking	barge	-arge	beautician	-ition
backed	-act	bargepole	-ole	beauty	-uty
backfire	-ire	bark	-ark	beaver	-iever

grazing	-azing	groaning	-oning	gutter	-utter
grease	-ease[1]	groom	-oom	guy	-y[2]
greased	-eased[1]	groove	-ove[3]	guys	-ize
greasing	-easing[1]	grope	-ope	guzzle	-uzzle
great	-ate	gross	-ose[1]	Gwen	-en
greater	-ator	grotty	-otty	gym	-im
great-grand-		grouch	-ouch	gymnastic	-astic
daughter	-ater[1]	ground	-ound		
great-		ground-breaking	-aking	**H**	
grandfather	-ather	grounding	-ounding	had	-ad
great-		group	-oop	hag	-ag
grandmother	-other	grouse	-ouse[1]	hail	-ail
great-grandson	-un	grove	-ove[1]	hailstone	-one[1]
Greece	-ease[1]	grow	-o[1]	hair	-are
greed	-eed	grower	-ower[1]	hairbrush	-ush[1]
greedier	-eedier	growing	-owing	hairdresser	-esser
greedy	-eedy	growl	-owl	hairdressing	-essing
Greek	-eak	grown	-one[1]	hairdrier	-ire
green	-een	grown-up	-up	hairdryer	-ire
greener	-ina	grub	-ub	hair-raising	-azing
green-eyed	-ide	grubby	-ubby	hairy	-ary
greenhouse	-ouse[1]	grudge	-udge	half	-aph
greet	-eat	gruff	-uff	half-brother	-other
greeting	-eating	gruffer	-uffer	half-sister	-ister
grenade	-ade	grumble	-umble	half time	-ime
grew	-ew	grumbling	-umbling	halfway	-ay
grey	-ay	grump	-ump	halibut	-ut
greyer	-ayer	grumpy	-umpy	Halifax	-acks
greyhound	-ound	grunt	-unt	hall	-all
greying	-aying	guarantee	-y[1]	Halloween	-een
grid	-id	guaranteed	-eed	Hallowe'en	-een
griddle	-iddle	guarantees	-ees	halter	-alter
grief	-ief	guard	-ard	ham	-am
grief-stricken	-icken	guerrilla	-illa	hammer	-ammer
grieve	-ieve	guess	-ess	hamper	-amper
grill	-ill	guessed	-est	hand	-and
grilled	-illed	guessing	-essing	handbag	-ag
grilling	-illing	guest	-est	handball	-all
grim	-im	guide	-ide	handbrake	-ake
grime	-ime	guided	-ided	handcuff	-uff
grin	-in	guiding	-iding	handful	-ul
grind	-ind[2]	guild	-illed	handicap	-ap
grinder	-inder	guilt	-ilt	handicaps	-aps
grinned	-ind[1]	guise	-ize	handicraft	-aft
grinner	-inner	guitar	-ar	handiwork	-ork[1]
grip	-ip	gull	-ull[1]	handkerchief	-ief
gripe	-ipe	gum	-um	handmade	-ade
gripped	-ipped	gun	-un	handout	-out
grit	-it	gunner	-unner	hands-on	-on[1]
gritted	-itted	gush	-ush[1]	handwriting	-iting
gritter	-itter	gust	-ust	handy	-andy
gritty	-itty	gusty	-usty	handyman	-an
groan	-one[1]	gut	-ut	hang	-ang

Index

impure	-ure	inside	-ide	Iran	-arn
in	-in	insider	-ider	Iraq	-ark
in-between	-een	insincere	-ear²	Irish	-ish
incense	-ence	insist	-ist	irk	-ork¹
inch	-inch	inspect	-ect	iron	-ion
incident	-ent	inspected	-ected	irritate	-ate
incline	-ine¹	inspection	-ection	irritated	-ated
inclined	-ind²	inspector	-ector	irritating	-ating
include	-ude	inspire	-ire	irritation	-ation
incoming	-oming	inspired	-ired	is	-izz
incomplete	-eat	inspiring	-iring	isle	-ile
incorrect	-ect	install	-all	Isle of Man	-an
increase	-ease¹	installing	-alling	isolated	-ated
increased	-eased¹	instead	-ed	it	-it
increasing	-easing¹	institute	-ute	IT	-y¹
indeed	-eed	instruct	-uct	Italy	-y¹
independent	-endant	instruction	-uction	itch	-itch
indirect	-ect	instrument	-ent	it'll	-ittle
indiscreet	-eat	insult	-ult	ITV	-y¹
indoors	-aws	insure	-ure	I've	-ive²
indulge	-ulge	insuring	-uring		
infect	-ect	intact	-act	**J**	
infected	-ected	intelligent	-ent	jab	-ab
infection	-ection	intend	-end	Jack	-ack
inferior	-erior	intending	-ending	jackdaw	-ore
infinite	-it	intense	-ence	jack-in-the-box	-ocks
inflamed	-amed	intention	-ention	Jade	-ade
inform	-orm	interfere	-ear²	jaded	-aded
informality	-ality	interfering	-earing	jag	-ag
information	-ation	interior	-erior	jail	-ail
informed	-ormed	Internet	-et	jailer	-ailer
informer	-ormer	interrupt	-upt	jam	-am
inhale	-ail	interview	-ew	Jamaica	-aker
inhaler	-ailer	interviewer	-ewer	Jamaican	-aken
inhaling	-ailing	introduce	-uce	James Bond	-ond
inject	-ect	introduction	-uction	jam-packed	-act
injection	-ection	intrude	-ude	Jane	-ain
injury	-y¹	invade	-ade	jangle	-angle
ink	-ink	invaded	-aded	January	-y¹
inn	-in	invading	-ading	Japan	-an
inner	-inner	invent	-ent	Japanese	-ees
innermost	-ost²	invention	-ention	jape	-ape
innocence	-ence	inventor	-enter	jar	-ar
innocent	-ent	investor	-ester	jaunt	-aunt
inquire	-ire	invitation	-ation	jaw	-ore
inquired	-ired	invite	-ight	Jaws	-aws
inquiring	-iring	invited	-ited	jaws	-aws
insane	-ain	inviting	-iting	jealousy	-y¹
inscribe	-ibe	involve	-olve	Jeep®	-eep
insecure	-ure	in-your-face	-ace	jeer	-ear²
insecurely	-urely	iota	-ota	jeering	-earing
insert	-irt	IOU	-ew	jelly	-elly
insertion	-ersion	IQ	-ew	jellybean	-een

mobile	-ile	mount	-ount	mutt	-ut
mock	-ock	mountaineer	-ear²	mutter	-utter
mocks	-ocks	mountaineering	-earing	mutton	-utton
mode	-owed¹	mourn	-orn	muzzle	-uzzle
moisturizer	-izer	mouse	-ouse¹	my	-y²
molar	-oller	mousetrap	-ap	mynah	-iner
mole	-ole	mousetraps	-aps	myrrh	-ur
molecule	-ool	mousse	-uce	myth	-ith
money	-unny	moustache	-ash		
moneybox	-ocks	mouth	-outh¹	**N**	
moneylender	-ender	move	-ove³	nag	-ag
moneymaking	-aking	moviegoer	-ower¹	nail	-ail
monk	-unk	moving	-oving	nail-biting	-iting
monkey	-unky	mow	-o¹	nailbrush	-ush¹
monsoon	-oon	mowed	-owed¹	naive	-ieve
monument	-ent	mower	-ower¹	name	-ame
mood	-ude	mowing	-owing	name-calling	-alling
moon	-oon	mown	-one¹	named	-amed
moonlight	-ight	MP	-y¹	name-dropper	-opper
moor	-ure	Mr Bean	-een	name-dropping	-opping
mooring	-uring	Ms	-izz	namesake	-ake
moose	-uce	much	-utch	nanny-goat	-oat
mop	-op	muck	-uck	nap	-ap
mope	-ope	mucky	-ucky	naps	-aps
moral	-oral	mud	-ud	nastily	-y¹
morality	-ality	muddy	-uddy	nastiness	-ess
more	-ore	muff	-uff	Nat	-at
moreover	-over¹	muffle	-uffle	nation	-ation
moron	-on¹	mug	-ug	nationality	-ality
morose	-ose¹	mule	-ool	nationwide	-ide
Morse	-orse	multimedia	-eedier	natter	-atter
mortar	-ater¹	multiplex	-ecks	naturally	-y¹
moss	-oss	multiplication	-ation	Nazareth	-eath²
most	-ost²	multiply	-y²	near	-ear²
motel	-ell	multiplying	-ying	nearby	-y²
moth	-oth	multistorey	-ory	neat	-eat
moth-eaten	-eaten	multitude	-ude	neaten	-eaten
mother	-other	mum	-um	neater	-eater
motherhood	-ood	mumble	-umble	neck	-eck
mother-in-law	-ore	mumbling	-umbling	necks	-ecks
mother-of-pearl	-irl	mummy	-ummy	nectar	-ector
motif	-ief	munch	-unch	nectarine	-een
motion	-otion	muscle	-ustle	need	-eed
motor	-ota	muse	-use	needier	-eedier
motorbike	-ike	music	-ick	needing	-eeding
motorboat	-oat	musician	-ition	needlecraft	-aft
motorcar	-ar	musing	-using	needlework	-ork¹
motorist	-ist	musk	-usk	needy	-eedy
motorway	-ay	Muslim	-im	neglect	-ect
motorways	-ays	mussel	-ustle	neglected	-ected
mould	-old	must	-ust	neigh	-ay
moult	-olt	muster	-uster	neighbourhood	-ood
mound	-ound	mute	-ute	neighed	-ade

Index